Shauna's courageous fight for God's will t[...]
beautiful beyond words. *A Fierce Love* is an a[...]
his strength, we can still choose to show love . . . even with a broken
heart.

LYSA TERKEURST, *New York Times* bestselling author;
president, Proverbs 31 Ministries

When author Shauna Shanks got the worst news a wife could get—that
her husband wanted a divorce—she pleaded with God, "Please just give
me one thing I can focus on! Just one word." He gave her two: *Endure.
Hope.* I urge you to read this remarkable story of one wife who decided to
lean completely on the Lord and to not give up, but to fight for her marriage. You will not be disappointed.

CHRISTINE CAINE, founder, A21 and Propel Women

This is so much more than the story of a faithful wife wooing her wayward husband back to their marriage. It is the story of a faithful God
wooing his wayward people back to his side. If you've ever wandered
or been wounded by someone who has, you will find great comfort
and encouragement in all the words Shauna shares. No matter what
the imposing mountain in front of you looks like—marriage, money,
sickness, or shame—you will learn from her example how God reveals
himself through life's impossible situations.

AMY LIVELY, author, *How to Love Your Neighbor
Without Being Weird*

Shauna Shanks takes us on a journey of what it's like to be faced with
an impossible situation, and to either do what makes sense in the eyes of
the world and those around us, or have the audacious faith that God calls
on us to have. *A Fierce Love* is a must read for everyone who has ever had
their faith put to the test in a big way.

CHAD VEACH, lead pastor, Zoe Church
in Los Angeles, California

Wow. Sometimes relationship miracles are the most amazing miracles of all. This is one of those miracle stories we need to know about. At its core, this is a story about a person's relationship with God as it is tested and navigated through one of the most severe crucibles of life. There were times in Shauna's story where I could hardly believe she was getting skewered and crushed by these emotional attacks again and again. And yet in the midst of those situations, she shares her vivid examples of God opening her eyes and directing her to dig in and use the principles of the Word of God and overcome by faith, even when it seems she is hanging on by a thread emotionally. I really love the battle-tested and practical examples she shares. For this reason, this book is a road map of sorts, but one that shows not just the way through to a miracle, but also the pitfalls of despair when one strays off the path—and how to course-correct by God's mercy and grace. We need to know stories like this exist—especially in this hour, when so many hearts are used to giving up and growing hard and cold. This kind of story restores hope in the power of God's love to overcome obstacles and shows love is worth fighting for, even when the situation seems to drag on without any reason for hope. God never leaves your side, and his Word and his Spirit will both work in and with you to strengthen you to see these amazing miracles happen.

TIMOTHY JORGENSEN, pastor; author, *Spirit Life Training*

# A Fierce Love

# Shauna Shanks

# A Fierce Love

## One Woman's Courageous Journey to Save Her Marriage

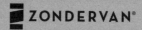

ZONDERVAN

*A Fierce Love*
Copyright © 2017 by Shauna Shanks

Requests for information should be addressed to:
Zondervan, *3900 Sparks Dr. SE, Grand Rapids, Michigan 49546*

ISBN 978-0-310-34753-8 (softcover)

ISBN 978-0-310-34846-7 (ebook)

*Cover design: Micah Kandros*
*Interior design: Denise Froehlich*

First printing April 2017 / Printed in the United States of America

To Micah—for your support and
willingness, without reservation,
to share our story.

To Aunt Jan and Shannon—for
journeying the trenches with me
and taking me to the paths.

For my boys: Josiah, Gabe, and
Judah—for praying every night
for "mommy to get her book published."
Thank you for your prayers.

# Contents

# Acknowledgments

This being my first book, I'm not sure if it's normal to cry through writing the acknowledgments, but I surely did! I am honored to have crossed paths with you all. Your contribution to this book is immense. Thank you. We truly did this together.

Russell and Shannon who were the first to tell me, "You should write that down."

John and Shannon Kellough, thank you for your spiritual covering. What an example you've given us to follow.

My very first editor, Angie Warner, who took on a project from someone she had never met before.

Leslie and Hattie, the first set of eyes to read my initial manuscript.

My editor Sandra Vander Zicht, for taking a chance on an unknown writer and championing this project from the very beginning. Meeting you at She Speaks was like a dream come true, and you continue to be such an inspiration to me!

Lori Vanden Bosch, whose feedback, advice, (and chopping!) took my original manuscript and masterfully crafted it to be a real book. Thank you!

David Morris, Tom Dean, and the whole Zondervan team for this opportunity to write. Your expertise has taught me so much through this process, and I am honored to be working with the best in the industry.

Robin Phillips, for your advice in the beginning and for being a quiet champion.

Lysa TerKeurst and the whole P31 team, for creating She Speaks to offer help to writers who have no idea what they are doing. Thank you for investing in women and making sure we are equipped to follow through with our God-given passions and talents. She Speaks was the avenue that started it all for this project. I have learned so much about writing through this ministry and have made many contacts and friends along the journey.

Amy Lively, my first writer-friend! Thank you for taking my phone call and walking me through those initial steps, and for your encouragement along the way.

My Pastors Mark and Nicki Pfeifer for coming along side of Micah and me and sowing into our family. It's an honor to serve with you.

Pastor Rick Cole and Capital Christian Center for being our second church home, whose presence is weaved throughout this whole story.

Blake and Kellie, friends who are also leaders.

Christine Caine, my spiritual coach! Your contagious passion for Jesus inspires me to go out and kick devil butt! You will never know how you encouraged me in the trenches as I listened to "Coffee with Chris" on repeat, teaching me to dream big, work hard, and trust that God will do what he said he'll do. Can we please go get coffee now?

Pastor Carl Lentz, Pastor Judah Smith, Beth Moore, Margaret Feinberg, and Jennie Allen for being voices to this generation and whose words I have repeated in this book. They may seem to be small mentions, but your impact is far greater than you could know. Thank you for being modern-day champions of Jesus through sermons, podcasts, books, events, and every single avenue you use to speak Jesus. It is so needed, and we are listening.

Jason Harper; mentor, pastor, friend.

Bryce Eldridge at Knowledge House Design and Marketing for helping me develop my platform and website and for keeping me on task in general.

Kim Potter for listening to every idea before it was translated on paper. We learned many of these lessons together, my friend. You're a treasure, seashell! Lyndsie, Alana, Crystal, Kristyn, and Rebecca, treasured friends, proof of my immeasurably more. What an honor doing life with you.

Jennifer, my forever friend, and the road trip that started it all.

# Chapter 1

# The Naked Man

SAN FRANCISCO, SPRING BREAK, 2003

• • •

*Adam and his wife were both naked, and they felt no shame.*

GENESIS 2:25

He parked the borrowed Audi TT at an overlook. Everything had been carefully planned. We strolled down Baker Beach, drove up Lombard Street, and visited the Palace of Fine Arts. We got to see Alcatraz and enjoy the famous bread bowls on the pier.

It was windy, the usual forecast in the bay. The sun was shining, creating nice breaks of warmth against the cold air coming off of the water. We took in the sights and smells of the sea lions as we paused to watch them play in the harbor.

The street performers were at their best. I'm sure there were more out than usual due to spring break. A man, wrapped head to toe in aluminum with his face painted completely silver, completed an act. I can't for the life of me think of what he was doing. I only remember that he looked amazing, as if he were straight from *The Wizard of Oz*.

The performers buzzed about the already crowded streets, seeking audience from anyone who would pause. There were musicians and street magicians. A fake cop even stopped me and gave me a ticket for "turning too many heads." I still have it in a trunk upstairs.

The experiences of the day were heightened only by the fact that I was finally with him, with Micah. We were nearing the end of a two-year, long-distance relationship. We only got to see each other a few times a year. I was not taking him for granted that day. I had come to visit him during spring break. We were attending college in separate states.

That day, I got to hold his hand, kiss his face, and finally look into his eyes. Those days were before texting and FaceTime. We relied on email and strategically planned phone conversations. (Really starting to feel old admitting that!)

* * *

We knew each other in high school. We had the same group of friends, but we had never really been friends with each other. It was right before senior prom and I had just broken up with my boyfriend of two years. I told my best friend, Jennifer, I wasn't going to go to prom. I didn't want to go with my ex-boyfriend, but going with anyone else would have been awkward.

Jennifer was appalled I was planning on ditching out of senior prom, so she kept trying to fix me up with someone. She went through everyone she could think of, and for each one, I had a reason I didn't want to go with them. I had just gotten out of a serious relationship. The last thing I wanted was to start another one. I was young! I wanted to relax, hang out, and just chill. Then she said, "What about Micah?" He had graduated the year before.

"Actually," I hesitated, "I would go with him."

I thought of him as the group goofball. He was super laid-back and funny. He was the one who made people laugh. I knew if I went with him it would not turn into anything serious. "Okay. I'll go with him" I told a giddy Jennifer.

After prom, I wanted to marry him.

We started dating after that, but we had already enrolled into separate colleges. He was headed to Sacramento, California, and I would attend Christ for the Nations in Dallas, Texas. After only four months into our courtship, we decided to give long distance dating a shot.

* * *

Around dusk, he led me underneath the Golden Gate Bridge. The lights from the city above us sparkled down upon the water. Waves smashed up against giant rocks that were scattered on the sandy beach. He hopped up onto one of them and reached out his hand to lift me up with him. I knew what was coming next. It had been the perfect day. This would be the perfect ending.

As he knelt down on one knee and buried his hand into his pocket, we heard a shuffling sound coming toward us. *Was that movement?* It was something coming toward us, fast. The sun had already started to set, making it difficult to see very far into the distance. Micah paused so as not to be interrupted by this ill-timed distraction. Coming quickly into view, I saw him. For many years to come we would affectionately call him in the retelling of this story, *the naked man.*

*Is he running toward us?* Technically this was a nude beach. But for heaven's sake, couldn't he see we were having a moment here? Plus it's *cold* out here! The naked man ran all the way to the rock where I was standing and Micah was kneeling. He reached out his hand, touched the rock, spun around, and ran back the way he had come, his behind bouncing all the way.

*Oh, San Francisco. How I love you.*

My ring was beautiful. It was perfect. I loved it. I loved him. I was finally engaged to the man of my dreams.

The next time the bridge would see us would be the mark of

our ten-year wedding anniversary. That visit would be in stark contrast to the first one. It would find us amidst a last-ditch attempt to salvage any remnants that may have been left of our marriage.

# Chapter 2

# The Start of Death

*Whoever tries to keep their life will lose it, and*
*whoever loses their life will preserve it.*

LUKE 17:33

I was excited. As creative director for the children's ministry at our church, I was being sent away to a conference for the weekend. *I was being sent away!* Thank God.

In addition to being a mom of three young boys, I also ran a small business making cakes from my home. I did weddings, birthdays, baby showers, and bridal showers—all things that take place on the weekends. So, weekends away did not happen often. Actually, I couldn't recall there ever being a time I was away from my children since having them!

My friend Crystal was also going to the conference. I was confident we could do all the conferency stuff while still getting in a good amount of much-needed goof-off time. We could hit up all the good local food places, window shop, and eat late-night snacks in bed!

Were there still shows on TV that were not on the Disney Channel? I would have no kids to wrestle or bathe for two whole nights! I would not have to cook, do one single load of laundry or dishes, or clean up one sticky mess on the floor. I didn't care what we did; this was vacation to me. Bring it on!

It wasn't until the night before the conference that I actually took the time to sit down and read over the itinerary. I blame this procrastination on being a mom to three kids. "Sit down and read time" is rare. I also call this my *Three Kids Card*. Laundry piled up? Dinner is late? Here's my *Three Kids Card*. Take a number and get in line. The littles take up most of my time and energy for now. Each task is interrupted by a dozen little demands and distractions that keep me seemingly running in circles most of the day. So even though I've been very busy all day, I've actually gotten very little accomplished. But at the end of the day, everyone is alive. *Patting myself on the back.*

As I sat in the quietness, with the itinerary in my hand, my excitement for the weekend was replaced with downright hysteria. The last night of the conference, my newly discovered favorite band was going to be there! They were scheduled to play the closing night of the conference. I called my husband to tell him the good news. He was excited for me because he was familiar with my newest obsession.

I had discovered the band All Sons & Daughters a few weeks before, when I had stayed up all night working on a wedding cake order. For some reason I had the old hymn "Come Thou Fount of Every Blessing" stuck in my head. I often set the laptop on the counter to listen to music while I work. (For this reason, our laptop has a pretty good coating of powdered sugar and shortening behind its keys. Oops.)

When I did a quick search for the hymn that night, the band All Sons & Daughters popped up on the computer screen. They had a cover of the song. I ended up continuing to click on their songs for most of the night.

Their music had such a worshipful tone. They were songs that caused me to pause, bow my head, and give in to a few tender moments with my Creator. My life, for the most part, was full of busyness, noise, and at times, chaos. These songs seemed to make all of that fade into the background and created a desire in me to just cozy up beside the One they were singing about.

*Oh yeah*, my soul seemed to say. Those sweet moments of worship seemed familiar but also far away. I recognized joy simply by connecting with my Creator, but I also felt a tinge of guilt too. The joy came from spending time with a friend I didn't see much, but the guilt ensued because I knew I left my friend in the first place. I reckon the sadness I felt was a result of not being a better friend. Little did I realize the significance of this night spent working and listening to these songs.

The songs stuck with me in the weeks to come. I added them to my running mix. (Which should have been called a walking mix because I had only recently decided to start running. To even call it light jogging would have been a great embellishment.) Even though the running wasn't a pretty sight, as I listened, something stirred within me.

• • •

The morning of the conference, Crystal's "mom van" arrived in front of my house, and off we went. We headed about an hour north, to the city of Columbus. We attended the workshops, explored vendor booths, and posed for pictures, wearing oversized glasses and floppy hats. We collected all the free giveaways and spent the very last dime of our eating allowance.

When the last night of the conference arrived, I had an expectation. I decided not to waste the evening. I knew God had been drawing me in and prepping me to spend time in his presence by teasing me with the songs I'd been singing that night in my kitchen. They had prompted a fierce desire in me to get closer to my old friend.

The fact that the All Sons & Daughters band was playing when I had only recently learned of them seemed like a pretty big coincidence. I decided to believe that God had booked them to be there just for me, and I was determined to meet him there. Besides, I was hardly ever without kids hanging off of me and rarely outside of the children's wing at church. Lord knew I wasn't giving him much time on my own. I was ready. I was going for it.

We had come with a team, and they had chosen seats on high-rise bleachers at the back of the room. It was the seating farthest away from the stage area. Where we sat, bright industrial lights shone brightly down on us. I thought the floor seating looked inviting, dark, and cozy, and I was overcome by a desire to go down there.

I knew I wanted to do some serious God-searching and I wouldn't feel so inhibited by watching eyes if I went closer to the stage. The lighting up front was dim and most of the people were standing, so I should've been able to blend right in without making any waves.

I stood up once the music started and was the only one doing so in my section. But I was overcome. I put Crystal in charge of my purse, excused myself from our row, and began to make my way through all the people.

I started to head down to the main stage area. The closer I got to the front of the ballroom, the more overcome I was. I had no idea what I was doing, but while I was still five or six rows back on a side aisle in the middle of nowhere, I suddenly knelt down and began to sob. Not a lady-like cry either. It was uncontrollable. Shoulders convulsing, snotty, messy, forehead-on-the-floor *sobbing*.

*What am I doing?* I didn't know. It wasn't *that* kind of service and I hadn't physically bowed down on my knees during a church service in years. At some point a woman briefly knelt down beside me and laid her hand on my back and patted as she prayed out loud, "Oh God, only you know what this woman is going through. . . ."

I knew I looked like a hot mess. I smiled to myself and thought, *Of course she would think something is deathly wrong by the scene I am causing, but I'm not "going through" anything. I just want more of Jesus. Nice, silly woman.*

Little did I know, that same night, things were already being put into motion to assure my death. The sentence had been "written down" and set into motion from that moment on. I guess Jesus took me seriously when I asked for more of him. I was about to get him.

I take comfort in knowing that he knew what was going to happen. He was drawing me into his sweet presence ahead of time, preparing me and holding me. He was with me every step of the way from that moment on.

● ● ●

It was October 14. I will always remember that. I had only arrived home from the conference the day before. I went for a "run" that evening and I was just so proud of myself for not collapsing into someone's yard. I felt on top of the world.

The kids were in bed, so I was preparing to reward myself by drawing a warm bath. Micah came in not acting himself. He said he wanted to talk, but then said, "Never mind. Just enjoy your bath first." Well, there's this common decency rule when talking to humans. You can't start something like that and not finish it. I remember being playful and sitting down to talk.

Things were good with us. I definitely wouldn't have called our marriage perfect. But good, sure. So I was completely caught off guard when Micah started speaking. I was laughing before I started crying. I laughed because I honestly thought he was joking. He was explaining that he didn't want to be married to me anymore. As he talked, my sweet husband disappeared and a stranger appeared. Serious. Cold. Cunning. He had planned this. It was an ambush.

He said he was not happy. He was not attracted to me, nor had he been for years. He did not love me. He didn't want to spend any more of his time with me. Didn't I want him to be happy? Didn't I feel the same way? I heard his words, but it sounded like crazy talk.

Over the next few days, he would continue to assure me of how little he thought of me. I felt like the little puppy in the movies that doesn't believe he is being abandoned by his owner, so the owner kicks it to get it to go run off into the woods.

His words paralyzed my heart. I was blindsided, yes. But it was quickly sinking in. I felt unbelievably stupid too. Yesterday I believed a happy reality. It was only a happy little lie.

I had never before worried about our marriage. He had never given me any reason to feel concerned. I did notice gaps in our marriage over the years and I did feel a lack of affection from him at times, which I had gotten used to because I thought that was just how he was. I just assumed he wasn't overly touchy-feely.

Micah had come from a very troubled childhood. I figured the lack of connection I felt at times was a result of that. He was never overly affectionate, but I thought that was his normal, and I never wanted to push him to be something he wasn't. Even so, I never felt unloved by him. I never expected this.

Yet now, this man with whom I had built a life, made promises to, and shared our children, opened his mouth and declared, "I do not love you." His words were a knife that cut into my soul. "I am not attracted to you." *He dug the knife in further.* "I shouldn't have married you." *He twisted it.*

When I tearfully remembered that the following month would be our ten-year anniversary he bluntly responded, "I know. I have wasted ten years of my life with you and I don't want to waste any more of my time. I feel nothing for you." These were the words that were the start of my death. The girl I was would be no more. She was already gone.

I couldn't have imagined this scenario in a nightmare. He said there was no one else. He just kept saying he wasn't happy and *didn't I want him to be happy?* I felt like a blooming idiot. I literally had no idea.

I had been happy in my fantasy world. I remember just not understanding. I even thought it would be better to have heard that I had been cheated on. At least then he would be leaving me for something, for someone. But nothing! I felt worse than nothing. It felt horrible.

It didn't make sense to me, and I felt hurt beyond words. He didn't just say, "I don't love you *now*." What I heard is that he didn't love me *ever*. He didn't just stop loving me at some point and then end our relationship. It was like he went back into time and pulled the rug out from under everything we ever had. He just simply took it all away. *Poof.* It was gone. Make-believe.

I started crying that night and cried for three days straight. I still remember those days and nights spent curled up in a ball on the couch. I didn't eat. I barely slept. I just cried.

It's difficult for me to recall the first night. I was heartbroken. My world was shattered. I was grieving the loss of my happy life and my little family. I knew I should have been hurting for our kids and the loss of their dad, but I couldn't get past my own grief. I still loved him. I just wanted to grab him, hug him, and kiss him like I always did whenever I wanted. I started to think of never being able to do that again and started to panic.

The thought of being deprived of his touch and his affection was too much. All I wanted was to touch him and be touched by him. I wanted him to embrace me and take it all back. But after "the talk," he changed toward me. He looked like my husband, but he was not. He was truly gone.

The next night I panicked. As I watched him prepare his things to leave, I made him sit down with our oldest son, Josiah, then eight years old, and tell him he was leaving. I didn't think he would be able to have that talk with him. I was wrong.

He recited some feeling-less something about "Your mother and I. . . ." I could only silently die from the other couch. *What are you doing?? Have you lost your mind? Our kids have no idea there could be a world where mommy or daddy could ever leave them. That's an option? And leave me out of it! Mommy nothing! This is all you,* I silently screamed.

He left to go for a run right after that. I was not ready to deal with changing our whole family dynamic in one evening, so when he came back I asked him to leave his stuff at our house and sleep there for the night until I could figure out my next move.

I'm not going to lie, those first few days I wanted to die. If I didn't have my kids to shield from all of it I would have crawled under a blanket and not crawled out. I had never really experienced a broken heart before. This was the first real personal trauma I'd ever had, and I felt like I could not pull myself together.

That first night when I lay awake crying, my mind was swirling. Sadness. Grief. Disbelief. Shock. *What do I do? What do I do without him? What about this big dumb house? I don't want to live in it without him! What about Josiah's school? Where will we go?*

*What do I do?*

# Chapter 3

# God Speaking

*And now these three remain: faith, hope and love.*
*But the greatest of these is love.*
1 CORINTHIANS 13:13

Finally, in desperation, I pleaded with God, "Please just give me one thing I can focus on! Just one word. Too many thoughts are ransacking my brain and I need to be calm and sleep." I had to get up with the kids in just a few short hours and I knew if I didn't sleep I would be exhausted all the next day. Maybe if I could focus on one word my mind would stop racing. "Give me something, God, *anything.*"

God gave me two words.

*Endure. Hope.*

Immediately my mind went to 1 Corinthians 13, The Love Chapter. I never would have gone there on my own. It sounded too cliché to me, too recitable. It's the chapter that is always read during wedding ceremonies. It seemed very common and over-used. I grew up a church kid. Sunday mornings, Sunday evenings, Wednesday nights, and any time the doors were open, my family was there. Us kids were even in Bible clubs where we were given prizes for memorizing popular Bible verses. So when I say I knew those verses, *I knew those verses. I know how to love, for goodness' sake.* That's too simple. Elementary.

Nevertheless, I was grateful for those words and for something to focus my attention toward. Immediately, I looked up the word *endure*. To endure means to suffer patiently. Deep breath. Relief.

*Okay. I can do that.* It doesn't sound fun, though. Especially since historically, "patiently" in God-years can mean forty years wandering around in the desert! Still, at least it's clear direction. It's something *to do*. I am thankful for that. I can wait. *I can endure.*

It's the hoping that will be the challenge. *Hope.* Hope is *believing for a desired outcome.* This outcome over which I have no control. Micah has made up his mind about me. I have been cut out. Like a dog that feels the hard blow of his owner's boot. It is setting in. I am being tossed aside and thrown away. "I am leaving you," he said. "I don't love you," he stated.

What if I hope and it never comes to pass? To keep hoping means to stay vulnerable. It keeps my heart soft when I'd rather it be hard and scab over. Then you can move on. I'd rather it heal and not be this raw, open, gaping wound.

Hope. Such a daunting thing to do when faced with such bleakness. *I will work on that one*, I vowed. After all, I only had two things to work on.

An amazing thing had happened, but in the trenches of my despair, I didn't recognize the miracle. I was so desperate to have something to hold onto that I reacted to the words he spoke, but I failed to pause and rejoice in the simple fact that God was speaking. It was amazing. But what was truly a wonder, and what hadn't happened much of my whole adult life, was that God was speaking, *and I heard him.*

I had been notorious for doing things and making decisions on my own and then asking God to bless those decisions. I didn't understand people who prayed and asked God for direction and then felt confident they had heard him. But my ability to hear God began that night without my even knowing it. In the desperate days and weeks ahead, I would come to depend on these words as the source of my life. God would continue to give me clear direction and never leave me alone.

I made a decision that first night not to love based on feelings. Feelings, as I had learned, can change with the wind, with the seasons. But love. It perseveres.

I was to continue to love Micah, taking any love I had been receiving from him out of the equation. That love had been replaced by betrayal, harsh and damaging words, and emotional abandonment. When faced with those things, God took me back to 1 Corinthians 13. *There it is. Do this.*

God's love is described in those verses, and he instructed me to love *his* way, not any way I was used to, and not based on feelings. There in those verses were written instructions that I could refer back to over and over again. I paused at every word and reflected on what it would look like for me if lived out this love as described.

"Love is patient, love is kind. It does not envy, it does not boast, it is not proud. It does not dishonor others, it is not self-seeking, it is not easily angered, it keeps no records of wrongs. Love does not delight in evil but rejoices with the truth. It always protects, always trusts, always hopes, always perseveres. Love never fails" (1 Cor. 13:4–8).

I replayed all the words I had read over and over in my mind. It is *not* jealous. Or rude. It is *not* provoked. It doesn't take delight in wrongdoing but rejoices when the truth is spoken. It *protects.* Love bears *all things, believes* all things. *Endures* all things. Love never fails. It Does. Not. Fail.

Only because of the state I was in did I begin to understand the enormity of the challenge in these Scriptures. To fully absorb God's message, I read the chapter over and over in every version I could find, including the Amplified Bible, "Love (God's love in us) does not insist on its own rights *or* its own way, *for* it is not self-seeking;

it is not touchy *or* fretful *or* resentful; it takes no account of the evil done to it [it pays no attention to a suffered wrong]. . . . Love bears up under anything *and* everything that comes, is ever ready to believe the best of every person, its hopes are fadeless under all circumstances, and it endures everything [without weakening]. . . . Love never fails [never fades out or becomes obsolete or comes to an end] (1 Cor. 13: 5, 7–8 AMPC).

*My goodness, this love is beautiful.* It is perfect. *Is it possible?* It must be, because God said it. And he had it written down. And he spoke it to me. I clung to these words. I wanted my husband back. God's way seemed like the way to go for me. The only way.

I was soon to discover that 1 Corinthians 13 was more than beautiful poetry.

# • Chapter 4 •

# *Crushing*

> *One evening David got up from his bed and walked*
> *around on the roof of the palace. From the roof*
> *he saw a woman bathing. The woman was very*
> *beautiful, and David sent someone to find out about*
> *her. The man said, "She is Bathsheba."*
>
> 2 SAMUEL 11:2–3

It was two weeks—to the day—after October 14, two weeks since Micah had asked me for a divorce.

Micah worked nights, but this was his night off. Even so, our sleep schedules were different. I went to bed late, thinking I was so tired that I would sleep well. Around 3:00 a.m., I woke up. Nothing had startled me. I couldn't fall back asleep so I got out of bed and walked into the living room to find Micah sitting on the couch with the lights still on. I cannot remember what we talked about other than it seemed like a good moment. He was speaking to me, first of all. That seemed promising. *How nice that I woke up*, I remember thinking. In those first few weeks, it was rare that he would be willing to talk to me.

But somewhere in that conversation the truth came out. He confessed there was someone else. He was having an affair. It was an odd mix of emotions I felt in hearing those nasty words. I instantly felt sick to my stomach. But the nausea quickly passed. I felt a strange peace. I knew he was watching my reaction carefully to see if I would stay the course to follow this absurd list I had told him about. *Love is patient*, I remembered. *Be patient,* I urged myself. *Love is kind*, I recalled. *Be kind.*

I ran through the list in my head until I got to hope. *Love always hopes.* I touched his shoulder that was next to mine. "This is not irreparable," I told him. "We can fix this," I hoped out loud.

These Scripture verses became a road map for me, ensuring that my reactions lined up with God's standard. The list kept me sane. I know now that acting like a lunatic when I received this information would have caused Micah to bolt out of our home immediately. But because God was teaching me how I should react by lining up my actions with 1 Corinthians 13, I was able to show grace and restraint, and Micah continued to stay in our home.

Deep down, I had suspected an affair. I wanted Micah to know that if there was someone else, I would understand. I wanted him to know I did not think our marriage disaster was all his fault. Before he opened up and confessed his betrayal, that same night I had admitted that I was once attracted to someone else during our marriage. I told him about Evan. It was when I worked at the hospital. Evan worked there too. I never talked to him, I just saw him around.

It actually was pretty embarrassing because whenever I saw Evan I could feel my face become flushed. I would try to be casual, act normal, and smile at him, but when he smiled back I would giggle like a school girl. My reaction was uncontrollable. His smile made me feel like I might melt into a big puddle on the floor. Every time I saw him I felt mortified because I knew he would smile at me and I would embarrass myself. My coworker friend who always walked with me thought this was hilarious, which of course caused an even bigger scene.

Evan must have known what was going on, but he never said anything. I told this to Micah that night. I explained that I never acted on that attraction. I had no intention of ever acting on it. I didn't even fantasize about Evan. My reaction to him seemed so involuntary. But I felt that Micah should know I understood the feeling of finding another person attractive and that I was able to keep that perspective.

I was reminded not to judge too harshly, when I myself wasn't perfect. I explained that I knew acting on feelings of attraction was wrong, and how I understood about taking my thoughts captive. I understood that despite what our feelings say, we have been given the ability to take authority over them. Our feelings are subject to us, not the other way around. It was after I shared that story with him, later in the night, he admitted to his affair.

The very next day, I was preparing to go for a run, and guess who I ran into? Yup, Evan from the hospital. He had spotted me and, with that big smile on his face, was waiting for me to pass by! I had not seen him in a few years, and even when I had seen him before, we never spoke. This day, however, *the day after* I learned of my husband's affair, when I was at my most vulnerable and emotional state, this man struck up a conversation with me. He talked to me like we were old pals. We ended up talking for several minutes. Turns out our sons were going to be on the same sports team and he had a question about a piece of equipment he needed to order. So he asked me for my phone number. *Seriously?*

Now, if you are a person who thinks all of this is one big fat coincidence, and do not believe in spiritual powers working against us, I cannot agree with you! I remember ending the conversation with him, getting into my car, and laughing. *Seriously, Devil? That was pretty blatant, even for you!* Someone was going out of their way and working overtime to destroy my marriage.

During the crisis in my marriage, I began to confide in Aunt Jan, Micah's aunt. She had become a near confidant. I called her before I even got home. When I first shared with her what God had told me to do regarding my marriage, she had warned me that the enemy would try and get to me. He might send men my way who could try and dissipate the resolve I had to fight for my husband. I literally laughed out loud when she said that. But the circumstances and timing of this chance encounter were too much to convince me otherwise. And I'd only felt a "crush" like that one time in our whole ten-year marriage! And here was this crush today, of all days, suddenly interested in me? *Nuh-uh.*

I knew even though I recognized it as a tactic of distraction from the enemy that I better get it out in the open. My husband had just told me he wasn't attracted to me and admitted to having an affair. I didn't even know if the affair was over. I was feeling pretty down on myself. Here this other person seemed interested, this person I had felt such an attraction to in the past. If nothing else, flirting would make me feel better and boost my confidence. Maybe that wouldn't hurt? *Maybe I'm not so bad after all . . . I deserve to be treated better . . . to be happy.* See where that could lead? My mind definitely went there for a minute.

I wonder how many "traps" like that are set and we willingly walk through them, calling them "an open door." Biblically, I had grounds for a divorce. I could have justified my actions of pursuing someone else. Except for, of course, the small issue that God had already spoken direction to me: *hope* and *endure.*

I could have pretended I didn't hear God, that I didn't know what to do. I thought about it. But he knew my heart. He would have known that deep down I knew the right thing to do and I rebelliously didn't want to do it because it was freaking hard. Had I hidden that conversation I had with that man, and kept it a secret, I could have been tempted to indulge in thoughts of possibilities. I could have been tempted to create a plan B in my head and eventually maybe go back there. When my feelings were hurt and my ego had been smashed, sure, I could've been tempted to turn down that path. But by telling Aunt Jan, I exposed that temptation, and its power was diminished.

For a few days after that, she asked me where my mind was, and whether I was being tempted. It was a relief to have that accountability. The enemy wouldn't waste his time on a tactic if it didn't work.

But at this point, I didn't waste too much time wondering what the devil was up to. I was too focused on what God was doing. And especially, what he was calling *me* to do. God had given me the most difficult assignment I'd ever been tasked with in my whole life: loving my husband.

# Chapter 5

# The Love Filter

*Let us not become weary in doing good, for at the*
*proper time we will reap a harvest if we do not give up.*
GALATIANS 6:9

Although I'd never had a specific worry about our marriage, I'd of course been aware that some spouses have affairs. I didn't give adultery much thought, though. Occasionally the subject of infidelity would come up in conversations with girlfriends. Sometimes, women, being so chatty and random, ask the "what if" questions. "What would you ever do if this happened?" sort of talk.

The way I pictured adultery was this: one partner, either intentionally or not, puts themselves in a bad situation, has a weak moment, and "it" happens. He or she is horrified and begs for the other spouse's forgiveness. At this point, the "victim" spouse has a choice to forgive or not. The thought never occurred to me that if Micah ever cheated on me he would not want me back. Obviously, he would feel terrible and beg forgiveness. *Right?!* He would want me back! He would want our marriage to work.

But that is not what happened. He did not want me. There was no remorse, no agonizing over a decision to stay or to go. The decision had been made. Out with the old, on with the new. That's how

I felt he saw me. Just the old to be out with! The whole situation seemed more than I could bear.

In the following days, I remained steadfast in my resolve to love Micah as God prompted me. At that time, a friend of mine who knew that Micah had asked me for a divorce, ran into him at a ball game. He stopped to talk to him and to let him know he was there for him if he needed anything. According to this friend, Micah casually replied that he was "on the fence" about his decision to stay with me or not. Another friend told me he said he was "weighing his options."

*Weighing his options?* Like does he want beef or chicken in his Chinese takeout? I am just an *option* now? This remark would plague me for weeks. *I. am. your. wife! You promised to honor me and to cherish me and to be faithful to me until we grow old. That was the deal, pal. How can you be casual and shrug me off as if you can take it or leave it?*

After I had patiently endured for a few more weeks, Micah maintained that he could not make a commitment to me because he didn't know if he wanted to stay with me and be faithful to me. He had clearly told me that he wanted to leave me, but I had asked him for some more time, to see if we could mend the relationship before rushing into the divorce. At that point, I was not even sure if he had broken off the relationship with the other woman.

He said he didn't want to leave the kids, but he felt nothing for me. He did not leave the house, but he told me he intended to move out. I did not know if that meant tomorrow or the day after that. I was literally taking one day at a time. About six months prior, Micah had decided to sell his pickup truck, so at the time our marriage imploded, we were still sharing a vehicle. This had previously been easy since he worked nights. But now, I figured not having a vehicle was the only reason he hadn't actually left the house yet. Although that may be a terrible reason not to abandon your family, I was thankful for the inconvenience and viewed it as God's meddling.

My husband was saying our marriage was over even as God was saying something else.

• • •

We had an old air purifying system in our house that used a filter. The filter is designed to let the clean air pass through while trapping the dust, allergens, and dander. In the same way, I purposed to "filter" my actions and reactions every day to follow 1 Corinthians 13. If my action fit the descriptions found in 1 Corinthians 13, it could "pass through." Those actions were allowed. For this reason I began to think of 1 Corinthians 13 as my Love Filter.

I had decided that my reactions, emotions, words, and responses should fit this guideline if I was to be truly obedient to God and follow this Scripture literally. I was the one who cried out to God for his help, after all. So I should at least do what he said.

If my reactions were not *kind*, or *patient*, or *hopeful*, or if they were *rude*, regardless of the wrongdoing done to me, they should not escape my mouth nor be acted upon. These were the rules, the standard to live by. I would go over the list in my mind. In many situations I found it necessary to stay silent on altogether. Micah would say something and I would bite my tongue to my natural instincts and instead speak hope.

Since God's Word is all of the things on the "allowed" list based on 1 Corinthians 13, I would speak Scripture freely. I would read verses and write them down to remind myself of the truth. I was not in denial of the messy reality that I saw before me. But I had been directed, you see, to have *hope,* and to *endure,* and to *love.*

When we would talk about what had happened, Micah expected a normal human reaction. He expected me to respond the way I would have acted before, on my own and without God's help. That was before I was given my Love Filter from 1 Corinthians 13.

Now I would not fly off the handle in a jealous rage or indulge in an angry rampage. My list specifically mentioned *not* to be jealous and angry. I *couldn't* lash out and spew mean words at him if I was to follow God's leading. That was rude, and rudeness was on my list of forbidden actions. I couldn't publicly bash him, speak negatively about him, or tear down his name. Love *protects*, and it said so on my list. I couldn't agree to sign divorce papers because that would be giving up. And the final word on my list was *perseveres*. Love perseveres. Love never fails. Love doesn't give up. I couldn't throw down an ultimatum and demand certain actions from Micah because patience was also on my list, and Micah wasn't yet in a place to be a husband.

This Love Filter may sound restricting. But it was absolutely liberating.

• • •

Now, let me please clarify this process of following the Love Filter. It wasn't as if God spoke this word to me one time and I was filled with unshakable faith. Rather, I became desperate for God's reassuring presence to carry me through. Like King Saul finding respite in David's music from the evil spirit tormenting him (1 Sam. 16:23), I was able to find calmness, a respite from the emotional chaos, in God's presence. So I sought it. Like an addict. Not once a day. All day. And he came.

In the midst of such heartbreak and uncertainty, a beautiful thing happened. I changed. Now I think it is impossible to stand and remain in God's presence like that and not be changed. How can one truly hear God's instructions and not cling to them? My husband's words had the power to destroy me. They should have. They did not. Instead, God spoke his own words over me.

I had known God before but never really as a constant friend. Psalm 25:10 says, "All the ways of the LORD are loving and faithful toward those who keep the demands of his covenant." His nearness to me at that time was overwhelming. Psalm 34:8 says, "Oh, taste and see that the LORD is good; blessed is the one who takes refuge in him." I had known this verse since my childhood. But only now did I truly grasp *how good* he is, and what his refuge is truly like. Those closest to me at the time kept remarking that I was in a "bubble." I should have been crushed, upset, and irrational. Instead, I was abiding in God's refuge. I would have never asked for the circumstances that led me there, but it was such an honor to be there now.

I was filled with hope. God's presence soothed me and healed me. That strengthened my resolve to do the right thing. He gave me strength—strength to face my husband and love him. It frustrated Micah and confounded him. And it started to change him. Or was it just the fierce hope I had that caused me to see a change, if only glimpses?

Micah continued to stay in our home. He said he was only staying for the kids and it was temporary, but I didn't care why he was there. God told me to fight for him and I viewed this as a victory. God had told me, "Do not leave him. Do not give up on him."

At first that was easy because I wanted my husband back and I genuinely didn't want to let him go. But as time trucked on and I saw how hard Micah's heart had become, I realized I was not fighting for just our marriage. I became convinced I was also fighting for Micah's soul. I believed that if he left our home he would spiral out of control.

The man was really pushing the boundaries of the Love Filter. He was looking for a way out. He was like a lion waiting to pounce on any excuse I would give him, hoping I would become weak in my resolve and just tell him to leave. I had a theory on why he hadn't left already. Maybe he wanted me to tell him to go. If I got frustrated enough and told him to leave, perhaps he would feel less guilt. As if at that point he could tell himself the separation was mutual. If that was truly his plan, I was going to make sure that never happened. If he left, I decided, it would be of his own doing. A separation would *not* be mutual.

Through the whole ordeal I kept insisting on that fact. I told him that I would not sign papers. I told him I would never ask him to leave our home. It was *his* home. We were *his* family. "I am your wife," I said again and again. "Even if you move on, I will never move on. I will never be with anyone else. I made you a promise." For better or worse. *And this was definitely the worst.*

Even still, Micah was *my person*. If I gave up on him, who would fight for him? I could not believe that leaving a wife who loved him and leaving his children, giving them up for every-other weekend visits, could lead him down any kind of path except that of destruction. He would be a shell of a man. The grass would not be greener on the other side. I became absolutely convinced that if he was not fulfilled by God, he could not be fulfilled. Satan was trying to destroy this man, I knew it.

As Micah remained in our home—all the while insisting our relationship was over—he mostly ignored me. When I tried to hug him or kiss him on the cheek, he would literally flinch as if the idea of being touched by me was disgusting. He would not hug me back. From time to time I would kiss him on the face and tell him I loved him and he would stiffen as if I were repulsive. He rejected me every day.

I knew Micah was toying with the idea of leaving me for good. Still, for brief moments he would seem conflicted and would say he wanted our marriage to work. I saw glimpses of hope in him, but mostly it was not pretty. When I tried to talk to him, there were times he would just swear at me and yell, slam the door in my face, and leave. That was how he dealt with me at that time. But God was ever present, whispering in my ear, "Listen to what *I* am telling you, not what he is telling you."

Hebrews 11:1 in the Amplified Version of the Bible reads, "Now faith is the assurance (the confirmation, the title deed) of the things

[we] hope for, being the proof of things [we] do not see *and* the conviction of their reality [faith perceiving as real fact what is not revealed to the senses]."

*Faith perceiving as real fact what is not revealed to the senses.* I loved that. I liked how this version mentions "the senses." Everything about my situation assaulted my senses. I *heard* Micah talking, rejecting me with his words. I *saw* him flinching and I *felt* his coldness. That was the reality at the time. It was the "real fact."

Yet God told me to perceive a reality beyond what I was experiencing. How could I give up?

I did have one person counsel me to kick Micah out of the house, "He needs to see what it is truly like without you and the kids." I knew this person meant well, but I couldn't do that. Micah had already given up, and I knew that if I gave up, there would be nothing left of us. I may have been the only one holding on to us, but I was holding on! On the days when I felt so weary of being rejected day after day, and I also felt like giving up, that was the scariest thought of all. I prayed for God to solidify my resolve to be obedient. And I hoped.

●　●　●

One particular day, I felt as if Micah felt sorry for me. He was annoyed too, because I was foiling his plans to start his new life guilt-free, but he felt sorry just the same. He was treating me as if I didn't fully grasp what was happening, or like I was in denial. I remember meeting his eye and saying, "I am not stupid, Micah. I know how you feel. I hear you. You have been brutally honest. But I also hear what God is saying, and I trust God more than I trust you. I hear what you are saying, but he is speaking too. I am listening to *him*, not to you."

I would explain again that God instructed me to love him and that's what I was doing. *Thank you very much.* Oh, it is so easy to love someone when they are loving you back, but it was quite the challenge during those days. I felt like Micah spent those weeks watching me, waiting for my big fat bubble to burst. Waiting for my resolve to fade, for me to "snap out of it" and the anger to set in. Waiting for me to realize that I hated him after all.

Sometimes it took every ounce of my strength to wait until Micah headed out the door for work, and then I would fall to my knees and figuratively shake my finger at God and say, "*You said! You* said, 'Wait and hope and don't give up on him' and here I am now, nothing more than an option!" In that place I had a choice. Was I going to believe what Micah was saying or follow what God was saying? I chose God.

It's a good thing too. Micah had already broken my trust. I realized even if by some miracle he changed his mind about me, there was nothing he could ever say or do to repair the damage he had done to me or to our marriage. If I had any hope left for the restoration of my marriage, I had to find my healing in God. He was my hope, my only hope. Only he could save me from crumbling. Craving love, I found it in God. Losing all trust in my husband, I found a better trust in God.

In contrast to the unfaithfulness of humankind, God was more than proving himself to me, and he was solidifying my faith that he was trustworthy—and that he loved me. I knew without any doubts that he was empowering me to live out the Love Filter. It was crazy to love like that! Yet God had told me to do something that confounded reason, then empowered me to do it.

He was not only helping me not to crumble but was strengthening my confidence in him each day. He was teaching me who I was in him and my value to him. I knew at that point, no matter the outcome, choosing to obey God was all I wanted. I wanted to please him simply because he loved me, and he was faithful to me.

And he was faithful to our children. Thank God, he protected our sweet boys.

# Chapter 6

# Suffer the Children

*They brought young children to him, that he should touch them: and his disciples rebuked those that brought them. But when Jesus saw it, he was much displeased, and said unto them, Suffer the little children to come unto me, and forbid them not: for of such is the kingdom of God. Verily I say unto you, Whosoever shall not receive the kingdom of God as a little child, he shall not enter therein.*

MARK 10:13–15 KJV

Without question, the worst night of my life was the night Micah planned to leave our home. Because not only was he going to leave me. He was going to leave our children.

Josiah was only eight years old. He is a very bright kid who excels in school. Being the only child for five years made him quite independent. Gabriel, my kindhearted middle son, had just turned four, and Judah, my loose cannon, had just turned two. Still too little to understand what was going on, the two littles had already gone to bed for the night.

When Micah sat down with our oldest son, Josiah, to tell him he was leaving, the conversation that followed was nothing short

of horrific. Micah's mind had "left the building." He was monoto-
nous and unfeeling. Josiah could not comprehend what Micah was
talking about.

It was almost an out-of-body experience for me; it seemed too
horrible to be real. The whole traumatic event ended with Siah
blocking the door with his little body and crying hysterically. He
wouldn't stop screaming, "Why? I just want to know why!" It was
heart-wrenching.

After Micah left to go for a run, Siah and I sat on the couch
together. At first I tried talking to Josiah using my own logic. I don't
know why I bothered. That was not effective in calming down my
child. At a complete loss for words and being devastated myself, I
know what happened next came from God. I explained the truth
as best I could for an eight-year-old to understand.

I leveled with him. "Do you know how at church you learn that
the devil is real and that he tries to trick people?"

"Yes," Josiah answered.

"Well, I think he is trying to trick Daddy. What can we do
when the devil tries to trick us?" I asked.

"Pray?" he responded.

"That's right," I said. "I'm gonna pray for Daddy, and you're
gonna pray for Daddy. And we will ask our friends to pray for
Daddy. Do you think God will answer all of those prayers?"

"Yes? He will . . . ," Josiah replied uncertainly.

Nodding my head I said, "Of course he will! Josiah, would
Mommy ever give up on you?"

"No."

"No! Do you think I would ever give up on Daddy?"

"No!"

At this point I raised the tone of my voice as if this whole thing
was ridiculous. This *was* ridiculous, and it was *not* happening. I
basically just told my eight-year-old, "Of course Daddy is not leaving!" (Even though Micah had just had this conversation with

Josiah moments before and was pretty adamant that he was.) But instead, I told my son, "We will just give this problem to God and he will take care of it for us, okay now?"

The conversation continued when he asked me how I knew the devil was trying to trick Daddy.

I said, "Because Daddy thinks he doesn't like me anymore. But I know that can't be true."

Siah looked confused.

"Do you know why that can't be true?" I prompted him.

"Why?"

I swatted at his leg as if he should already know. "Because I'm awesome!" I answered. "How could he not like me?" I made a silly face.

With that, the evening that began so traumatic and hopeless was turned around. Josiah smiled and even gave me a few laughs. I seemed to convince him that everything was going to be okay and I think in that moment, without even realizing it, I showed God my faith. Just a sliver was all that was needed. The only thing that could have been worse for me in that circumstance was for Siah not only to lose his dad, but to lose his faith in God.

If God hadn't come through for us, Siah's little budding faith could have been discouraged. I believe God knew my risk in talking to Siah with such faith and with so much on the line. It was audacious and presumptuous. I believe it moved God. I remember sending Siah upstairs to take a shower and I said to God, "Well, that was very presuming of me. You have to move now. It's all in your court. I just told Siah it's all on you." And it truly was.

Although that evening with Josiah is a horrible night to think about, what gives me comfort is knowing that Josiah's faith in God was increased that night. What did he learn? Satan is real, yes. He tries to trick us and destroy us. But God is also real. God is bigger. God is stronger. When we need something, we can go to God in prayer. We can trust him. He is able. He is faithful. The kingdom of heaven *belongs* to our children. We need them operating in faith too!

I know children whose suffering lasted longer than Siah's one night of devastation. I recently and helplessly watched as one of my best friend's marriage collapsed. One of my sons and her son are best friends. Her husband was having a secret affair with another woman for a long time. When my friend finally found out, they began going to counseling.

He said he had ended the extramarital relationship, but it became clear a few months later that he had not, nor did he have any intention of doing so. He ultimately asked his wife, my friend, to just let the affair continue while they remained married.

Obviously, this proposal was unacceptable for her and it became a very toxic relationship for my sweet friend. It was heartbreaking to watch her move their two kids out of their house and into a small apartment. One of her children took it particularly rough, as expected. His little world had been shattered.

Not for one second do I think that relationship failed because of any lack of faith on her part. My heart in telling my story is only that, it's *my story*. I had already heard orders from the Lord to hang in there and onto my marriage. My friend did not. She had her own obedience to walk through.

Regardless of our different approaches, my friend and I both landed at the end with the same conclusion. God is faithful, always. He not only takes care of us, but he takes care of our kids. Beyond the outcome of our marriages, God is concerned for the children. He makes them his business. And you can take comfort in knowing that if God is making something his business, he will indeed take care of it. He is so faithful. We prayed for peace, for wholeness and healing over our children. We prayed for God to mend their broken baby hearts.

We were finding out we could trust him. He created the whole universe. Can't he then also hold our little ones?

## • Chapter 7 •

# One-Way Glass

*For now we are looking in a mirror that gives only a
dim (blurred) reflection [of reality as in a riddle or
enigma], but then [when perfection comes] we shall
see in reality and face to face! Now I know in part
(imperfectly), but then I shall know and understand
fully and clearly, even in the same manner as I have
been fully and clearly known and understood [by God].*

1 CORINTHIANS 13:12 AMPC

I've never been imprisoned. I mean, actually imprisoned with chains and locks. But on those blurry days after October 14, I was in agony. It was an experience that made me feel as though I'd been arrested on some unknown charge, hauled off to prison, and thrown into solitary confinement. I was brought to a gray cell of suffering against my will, kicking and screaming, and held there without explanation. My heart broke as all the people I loved the most were in jeopardy and I was stuck and helpless in that stupid room. I wasn't sure if I would ever be able to get back to my family or if I could save them.

I was intimidated, scared, and alone. All I could see were the plain gray walls around me in the room where I was being held.

All I could feel was my pounding heart and the gaping coldness of feeling alone. The only thing that seemed real was my fear and heartbreak. It appeared hopeless.

When I finally felt well enough to explore my new surroundings, I noticed a mirrored wall. Not a true mirror, just a dim reflection where I could see myself and what a terrible state I was in. The image was blurred and grainy, but I could see that my eyes were swollen from crying.

When the door finally opened, it brought not friends nor even lawyers, but interrogators. *You will not get your family back. You are alone, powerless. You are not strong enough for this task.* The interrogators had a job to do. It was to make sure I was squashed, annihilated. The interrogations were relentless. Because of what I had to endure in that room, I knew I would not make it out intact.

I could only see what was in front of me, three gray walls and a tarnished mirror-wall. And somehow that mirror became my lifeline. When my tormentors would leave me to myself, I began to sense I wasn't alone. I crept up to that mirror, started to tap it, to try to see through it. I began to feel that everything around me was a facade, an illusion. I became convinced there was more to my situation than what I could see.

My eyes fixed on that mirror. It was dim and scratched and blurred, but it was all I had to look at. Yet deep inside my soul I thought I saw something else. Another reality was making itself more and more present even though I couldn't see it with my eyes. I knew that God was behind that mirror. And even though I couldn't see him, he could see me.

I began hearing a quiet voice telling me, "Get up." I felt like I was being watched, but in a way that was comforting. Knowing that I was being watched made my actions feel momentous. Somehow I sensed that I had some agency, some power after all. I felt that the way I reacted to the situation could change everything. I was being tested by fire, a searing flame that burned my soul. But it was a purifying and necessary testing.

I began to find strength in my weakness. When the tormentors made their daily rounds, I became convinced they were only making me stronger. Yet I was still being held in the room of the three gray walls and a wall of one-way glass.

• • •

One-way glass is obviously named for its function. It is designed so people can see from one side but not from the other. From inside the interrogation room, you can't see what's behind the glass. But behind it, indeed, people are there. They are walking around watching, talking, eating, living. They are just behind the glass. The fact we can't see them from the side we are standing on doesn't negate their reality one bit.

Being on this earth and being faced with all the heartbreaks and challenges that confront us during our time here can be paralyzing, like being stuck in an interrogation room. We believe in what we see right in front of us, which is limiting, constraining, frustrating, and even at times, tormenting. We can't see into the spirit world. We do not have the privilege of peeking behind the walls and seeing into another reality that exists—another realm that's behind the glass.

Yet behind that one-way glass a glorious spirit realm exists, a world that changes and is formed when people pray to God and he speaks forth his answer. I began to see that there were two realities.

Reality number one was the mess staring me in the face every day, where Micah's heart was turned against me with plans of leaving and splitting up our family.

Reality number two was the glimpse I was getting into God's reality, where God had declared that love wins. Of course, my day-to-day reality did not yet line up with God's reality yet, but I trusted it would. Why would you need faith if you could see the outcome?

Still in the trenches of my battle, I received an email from my friend Kristyn. It read, "Would you fight differently if you already knew the outcome? Would you stand stronger if you knew you had already won? Would you press on? Keep going? Because the war over his soul has already been won. It's not up for auction." Then she said simply, "Stay strong."

The day before receiving this text from Kristyn, I had confronted Micah about some things. He was living in the house and saying he wanted to work on things, but he didn't actually seem to be working on anything. He was cold to me and showed me no warmth at all. He was giving me no time or attention. He would not even touch me.

I confronted him about this and told him that it seemed to me he must still be holding on to his plan B. He was fantasizing about the other woman, I knew it. He was scheming up his escape plan. That was the only thing that made sense, that could explain his actions toward me. He admitted I was right in my perceptions. He wasn't apologetic. He actually threw it in my face. He admitted he was really just at the house with me out of duty.

*Nice.*

That was my reality at the time. As much as it hurts to even write that, it is important for me to explain the reality I was seeing. I don't want you to think that since it all worked out in the end, that I didn't go through a time of coming eye-to-eye with the enormous mountain that stood in the way of God's reality for my life.

Sometimes the reality the world lays out for us is one with little hope or promise of a future. We feel trapped and helpless, with nothing more than bleakness in our view. No wonder so many people give up! If we go by what we are told and by what we see, it really is hopeless! But God *behind the glass*, he was speaking too, remember? He can be very persistent. He persuaded me to believe in his words that had already been spoken. He had already set out to form this reality that I just couldn't see yet. He was about to move my mountain. What I knew was this: *I couldn't give up.* God's reality for me was *en route.* Soon enough, this reality on earth *had* to come into alignment with God's reality because God had already spoken his word. There is no power on this earth like the power of God's spoken word.

Remember, God's spoken word is so powerful he created *existence* with it. Genesis 1:2-3, "Now the earth was formless and empty, darkness was over the surface of the deep, and the Spirit of God was hovering over the waters. *And God said,* 'Let there be light,' and there was light" (emphasis mine). Read the rest of the chapter to see what else God did with his spoken word! When we grasp the power and authority that resides in God's spoken word, that's when faith kicks in.

And God had spoken to me in the quiet. He told me to hope and endure, and I did not believe God would send me on a goose chase. I believe he asked me to hold on to hope because he knew my marriage was restorable. (Likewise I believe that there are many parents and grandparents wildly praying for rebellious or addicted children and grandchildren, who can also relax in God's certain promises.)

As a daily reminder of hope, I scrawled these words across our bathroom mirror: *Faith moves mountains,* based on Matthew 17:20. Since Micah didn't move out of our house, he saw those words every day. Most importantly, I saw it; God's promise was right in front of my face, reminding me of something I learned in the interrogation room: If God speaks something, his word is good.

I can trust in that. I can rest in it. I can wait on it. It doesn't matter if I can see it or not. I can trust in what he has spoken to me more than I can trust what I see with my own eyes because another reality *does* exist and it's a spiritual one. This place we can't see is where strength is kept. To get it, one needs to look into the one-way glass. One needs to splay her fingers against the window, press her nose against the glass, and pray unwaveringly, seeking out God who is on the other side and is waiting for us simply to ask, so that he can supply us with everything we need.

. . .

Something haunts me when I think of that interrogation room. I think I am haunted because of you, dear readers. Which of you are in a place of struggle and need to know not to trust your own eyes? This is the question that haunts me, and compels me to keep writing despite any other hesitations I have. . . .

*What if I had given up because all I saw was a gray wall?*

# Chapter 8

# Blatant Indifference

*These are the ones I look on with favor:*
*those who are humble and contrite in spirit,*
*and who tremble at my word.*
ISAIAH 66:2

Early in November I gave Micah my wedding ring back. I had heard a word from God to love Micah, hope and endure, but I became exhausted from Micah's nonchalant attitude toward our relationship. I was really giving everything I had in an effort to save us, and at the time, I felt as if he was doing nothing. I was getting ready to go for a run one evening and I was trying to talk to him and he was ignoring me as I talked. In frustration and anger, I took off my ring and thrust it into his hand.

"When you are ready to give me this ring back, I will be here," I said. "I don't see you doing anything to fix this. I don't feel like you want to be here or like you want to even try to make this work. I can't do all the work. I want to be with you, but that's not enough. It takes two. I want to wear this ring. But wearing it with no commitment from you feels worthless. You have broken this marriage! If you want it back, you will have to ask for it!" With that, I ran straight out the door, my heart pounding. *What have I done?*

This whole story started with brokenness. In the very worst days, the initial days after October 14, I kept listening to a song by All Sons & Daughters called "Brokenness Aside." It speaks of how we let God down, how we run from him and lie to him, but yet he takes our brokenness and makes it beautiful.

It would have been easy to pin our marriage crisis on Micah, on the most obvious problem at the time: infidelity. It also would have been wrong. As I listened to "Brokenness Aside," I became heartbroken to realize my *own* failures and shortcomings. I discovered the sin in my own heart that had contributed to this situation. I was not blameless. I was not one to be casting any stones.

One particular night, I wrote in my journal about how unbearable it was for me to witness the way Micah was acting. That night, Micah had been sitting on the couch across from me, watching football carefree, yelling at the screen and casually playing on his phone like nothing was amiss. Just like any other normal day. He acted completely unaffected by the breakdown in our relationship, and that hurt beyond words.

Here sat this person who had stood at an altar and professed to love me. Yet his behavior proclaimed an attitude of blatant indifference toward me. Those are the actual words I wrote down in my journal, "Blatant indifference." It was as if he couldn't care less one way or another about me. Not even one little tear because our ten years together were probably over. Nothing. Not one emotion. Just indifference.

Only a few days later God revealed to me that he himself had the same complaint against me. It wasn't just the last few days that I held this attitude, but rather the last several *years*. "What was the term you used?" God asked me. "Blatant indifference?"

I heard God say to me, "You made a commitment to follow me, serve me, and love me. You surrendered and dedicated your life to me. You professed to give yourself over to me, to use your life for my glory, to be passionate about me, and spend time with me. And what do you do? You fill up your time with complacency and laziness. None of the things you do matter apart from me. Yet all the while you ignore me. You confess with your mouth that you love me, but you are acting toward me just like Micah acts toward you. There is no difference. You are living here, showing me no affection. No time. No attention. You are blatantly indifferent."

*Ouch.* That message pierced my heart. I was wallowing that Micah had hurt me, but I had done the same to God. *I was a sinner.* I had been so unfaithful, maybe not in my marriage, but to God himself.

My unfaithfulness is what had been the most wrong in my past, in my marriage, and in my promise to God to live for him. When I turned thirty, I was not exactly in the best place of my life. I was embarrassed by what I had become. I wasn't anything too terrible on the outside, like a murderer or arsonist, I just hadn't really become . . . anything.

I had a problem with Netflix bingeing. I have this one memory of staying up until two or three in the morning watching *Mad Men.* I knew I was going to be deathly tired the next day. But I didn't want to go to sleep. I wanted to stay awake and be entertained. Too soon tomorrow would come and I would have to start the day all over. I didn't want to do that. I was overwhelmed with my life, a tad depressed, and bored. I had gained a little weight so I stayed up lying on the couch watching TV in my husband's old night pants. My hair was a mess and my makeup was nightmarish, smeared. My house was a disaster. I just didn't care. I felt sorry for myself. I don't know why, but I did. In hindsight, I can see I was unfulfilled.

When my husband woke up from sleeping in after working third shift, I met him eagerly. Not because I was eager to see him or do anything worthwhile. I just wanted to sleep. He was up, so tag! You're it! I left him with no lovely greeting, *how was your night?* Just, *here's this disaster of a house. I'm out.* I was disappearing.

The look on Micah's face is burned into my memory. He told

me to go ahead and get a nap, but the look in his eyes made me feel ashamed of myself. I knew by being so lazy I was being selfish. He was disappointed in me. Not because I wanted to nap, but because he saw it too—I had given up. I had very little passion anymore. I remember passing a mirror and getting a good glance at myself. *Gross,* I remember thinking at my own image. But then the feeling passed. I really didn't care.

I wasn't living life to the fullest. I don't know when everything began to slow to a careless halt, but the brakes of caring had been turned on for some time. I had given my heart to Jesus as a little girl, even doing missions work in my teen and college years, but clearly by the time I hit thirty I wasn't exactly up there with any of the great saints yet. I wasn't trying to do much with my life. I was watching *Mad Men.* That's what I was doing.

Now, to some this may not seem like that big of a deal. I was still a good person, after all. I took good care of my kids, I volunteered at my church. But this lazy and passive behavior became corruption in my life. Revelation 3:15 addresses this, "I know your deeds, that you are neither cold nor hot. I wish you were either one or the other!" If you keep reading that same passage you'll find that the consequences of these "not a big deal" sins are pretty severe. In fact, it turns out lukewarmness, or laziness, actually is a really big deal to the Lord.

It hurt to hear God use my own term, "blatant indifference," about myself, but it was true. These revelations turned out to be the kindest thing he could have done for me. Do you know what it did? It took my eyes off of Micah. I started searching into my own self, realizing how far from God I had traveled. I stopped feeling so hurt that Micah had hurt me and instead felt burdened that I had done this to my God. I felt like a hypocrite if I let myself despise Micah for doing something that I myself was guilty of on a much more significant scale.

Had my eyes stayed on Micah at the time, I would have been

sorely disappointed. If I would have allowed myself to stay the victim in the story, I wouldn't have uncovered the source of a pretty major problem—myself! I wouldn't have been able to be changed. As our pastor said all the time, "God can't heal what you don't reveal."

God had just shone a giant spotlight on my soul and revealed to me areas in my own heart that were festering with sin and, in turn, spilling over into my marriage. I had to take responsibility here. Not for all of it. But for my part in it. That was enough to keep me busy.

My sin may have looked different than Micah's, but it was still sin.

One day, I wanted to tell Micah about the song "Brokenness Aside" and everything it meant to me. I imagined he thought I hated him and that I was appalled by his horrible behavior, and I wanted him to know otherwise. On one occasion as he was walking away from me I called out to his back, "Do not think I am thinking all of these terrible things about you, because I am not. God is keeping me too busy working on my own self for me to think about all the wrong that you are doing."

He ignored me. That is pretty much how he dealt with me at the time, so I had no idea what was going through his mind. Later he told me that my words affected him. He thought I would respond to his words in self-defense as I usually did when he came at me with accusations. But now, as God shined his glorious light on my flaws, I could only respond to Micah one way when he voiced a complaint against me. I would stare at him, mouth agape. "You are right. I have no defense. I am that. I did do that. I am so sorry for the role I have played in causing this." And I truly was.

That's why I had to die to the girl that I had been. I had two lives: My life "after" and "before." The life I had before was one of settling, of apathy. I was only sleepwalking. I was alive, but there was no adventure or passionate seeking of God in that life. I couldn't be that other person anymore. I had to be reborn. I was a believer in Christ before and I knew God loved me in my "before" life, but I had squandered this precious and limited time on earth. Too complacent, I lived quite comfortably with sin in my heart. I hid it and pacified it and lived, for the most part, completely in denial that it was there.

I felt very thankful for the grace in this terrible circumstance; I was jolted awake. Because of this grace I woke up and sought God. I was rejuvenated, alive, determined, and in love.

Of course I didn't realize I had been sleepwalking until I woke up. Only when God's presence showed up did things come to life again. The spotlight made things clearer. Scriptures I'd heard repeatedly, suddenly came to life. God's presence met with me in my living room. Almost tangibly. When I had lost everything, I had to trust in God to get any semblance of my life back. In response, I saw his faithfulness to me. I experienced his grace, his forgiveness. And it changed me.

I felt like I was on two honeymoons. One was with my Creator, God. My passion for him had returned. I desired once again to fully serve him and be in his presence. I was content just to seek that all day. Yet I also was on a honeymoon with my husband. True, for the moment, it was a one-sided honeymoon, but I was falling in love with him again even still. I had been given a brand new love for him. A selfless and more perfect kind of love. It was exhilarating. With God's love in your heart you feel empowered enough to conquer the whole world. Love always wins.

Even in the moment, I realized God's amazing power in this. This Love Filter I had come to depend on, this peace, this confidence, this amazing work God was doing in me was against my usual nature. I was honestly surprised by this resolve I had found and the fierceness of my love for Micah. I did not previously have such fierceness in my heart for this man. I felt a conviction, an urgency, a determination to love him. It was overwhelming. It was as if God was giving me just a taste into his own heart of how he must feel about Micah, and each of us. It was an experience that leaves me in awe thinking about it even now.

The thing about "dying" to yourself as a believer in Christ is, like Christ, you get raised back up! In Galatians 2:20 ESV, Paul explains, "I have been crucified with Christ. It is no longer I who live, but Christ who lives in me. And the life I now live in the flesh I live by faith in the Son of God, who loved me and gave himself for me."

I found that when I was humble and broken before God, being completely honest and at the end of my rope with myself, God stepped in. Being brokenhearted, not only by my circumstances but also by the realization of the sin that was present in my life, brought me to a place of humility—the best and safest place for me to be. Psalm 34:18 reads, "The Lord is close to the broken-hearted and saves those who are crushed in spirit." How could I have truly known the severity or the comfort of this verse without going through a broken heart?

Can you imagine what it is like to be near to God? Truly near him? I would not trade that nearness in for a thousand faithful years with my husband, for ten years without any problems. There is no way to understand the nearness of God as your comforter other than through brokenness and suffering. At least I had not found it. I had known him in many ways, but knowing him as the comforter was new to me. And I would not trade these treasured moments with my Creator for anything in this world.

## • Chapter 9 •

# *Breadcrumbs*

*Whether you turn to the right or to the left, your ears will hear a voice behind you, saying, "This is the way; walk in it."*

ISAIAH 30:21

God's faithfulness remained steadfast to me with each step. When I struggled or felt lost, he sent me breadcrumbs, letting me know I was on the right path. *This is the way, keep walking,* they seemed to say. He confirmed that I had indeed heard his voice correctly and then urged me to keep going.

The first breadcrumb came in the form of a text message. I will never forget that day. My friend Leslie had ordered some cupcakes for a fall harvest party at work, so the aromas of pumpkin spice and caramel apple wafted through my kitchen.

The night before, I had learned of Micah's affair, so as I was baking in my kitchen, although I had already been utilizing my 1 Corinthians 13 Love Filter for a few weeks, I was now bearing a new raw, open wound. Each day I had been very intentional about keeping my mind and thoughts on God, but now with this new information, it was even more important to do so. If I didn't, I would be tormented, tempted to panic, give up, grow depressed, and sink into a place of despair.

In my kitchen that day, I was in that place of temptation. I felt torn between really wanting to believe God and do what he said, and allowing myself to fall apart. Sometimes you just want to throw yourself a well-deserved pity party, you know? But I knew that choice would be destructive and counter to Scripture. It was a constant battle of choice in the minutes and hours of each impossibly long-passing day.

When Micah told me he wanted to leave me, one of the first decisions I made was to not tell my family about what was going on. I felt like God told me to lean on him and him alone, and he would be all I needed. Also, I thought that if God did change Micah's heart, and all of my family knew what he had done, it would make it that much harder for him to return to me. I felt that even if they could accept him back, it would never be the same. I didn't want to create any extra obstacles in case by some miracle Micah changed his mind.

Yet that afternoon, I had my finger placed on my mom's name on my phone. Overcome with grief, I thought, "This is too much. It's just too much to ask me to go through this alone." Then I made my choice: obedience. I set the phone back down on the counter, and I turned to God.

I prayed, sharing honestly about how much I was hurting. My heart was broken and the uncertainty of it all made the situation worse. I longed to have my husband back. I wanted to have hope. I wanted to believe restoration was possible, yet it was so obvious Micah's heart had left me. He was not choosing me.

These were the thoughts that were swirling around in my head when the beep of my phone interrupted them. It was a screenshot from Aunt Jan, who had randomly decided to share her morning devotion from *God Calling*. It even had the day's date, October 30, printed on the page she sent me:

### THE HARDEST LESSON

*And now, Lord, what do I wait for? My hope is in*
*You. Deliver me from all my transgressions; do*
*not make me the reproach of the foolish.*

PSALM 39:7–8

Wait, and you shall realize the Joy of the one who
can be calm and wait, knowing that all is well. The last,
and hardest lesson, is that of waiting. So wait.

I would almost say tonight, "Forgive Me, children,
that I allow this extra burden to rest upon you even for
so short a time."

I would have you know this, that from the moment you placed all in My Hands, and sought no other
aid, from that moment I have taken the quickest way
possible to work out your salvation, and to free you.

There is so much you have had to be taught—to
avoid future disaster. But the Friend with whom you
stand by the grave of failure, of dead ambitions, of relinquished desires, that Friend is a Friend for all time.

Use this waiting time to cement the Friendship
with me and to increase your knowledge of Me. [1]

To me, it was as if the Savior himself stood in my kitchen and
handed me a personal letter. The timing was perfect. The wording was perfect. He had already told me to wait, not to give up.
This devotion gently confirmed that, and my spirit was instantly
refreshed. There was no way I would give up now. I referred back
to this devotion many times that day and every day for the weeks
and months ahead until I could recite it.

The second paragraph touched my heart so. The God of the
Universe acknowledged my pain. *The God of the Universe acknowl-*
*edged my pain!* That was healing for me. For him to say to me, "I'm

working on this as fast as I can for you," was amazing to me. Just imagine. The God of Angel Armies was concerned with my business and was sending me this letter. Working on this with me, for me. It boggled my mind.

"Sought no other aid" confirmed for me that I was right to keep myself separate for a bit and gather my advice from God's own hand rather than getting lost in the clamor of other people's opinions of my crisis. He wanted to teach me that he was enough and he was capable. Not only did he acknowledge how hard it was to confide in only him, but he noticed and blessed my small morsel of obedience. I was astonished.

Even the last paragraph spoke to me. "But the Friend with whom you stand by the grave of failure, of dead ambitions, of relinquished desires, that Friend is a Friend for all time." Although I knew that the "Friend" spoken of was Jesus, I saw my husband in those words. I had grieved, and I watched as my husband and best friend was drained of life, desire, and ambition. We stood at the grave of our failed marriage, and on his side, he had no ambition to revive it. Instead, he seemed to have relinquished all desire for me and all the desire he once had to serve the Lord.

I thought I had lost him.

Then God said "that Friend is a Friend for all time." I took these words as a promise. Micah would come back to me and our friendship would last. This suffering would make us stronger. Up until this point, I only knew to hope and endure. But God never technically promised that my marriage was going to last. I was being obedient, but I didn't presume that I knew the outcome of our trials. I knew God wanted to show Micah his own love and that was the most important thing. But that afternoon I felt relief. I knew after that, no matter how ugly it got, Micah would be my friend for all time. God told me so. And while I waited, I would cozy up next to this great, amazing God I had, and I would try to learn more about him.

After I received my first breadcrumb that afternoon, I sank down into a ball on the cold tile of the kitchen floor and sobbed. I tried to wrap my head around what I had just experienced. How could this God who spun the planets be so *personal* to me? Why did he concern himself with my struggles? My broken heart was all-consuming to me, but what was it to a God who placed the foundations of the earth and who ruled the skies? Yet here he came into my kitchen that day. He spoke to me. He cared for me. He hand-delivered me a message.

Overwhelmed at his ability to heal me with just a few words, I allowed myself to cry. I didn't rush it, and I didn't want it to end. I hadn't been receiving love in the past few weeks, but there on my kitchen floor in a heap beside my corner cabinet and surrounded by God's presence, I received love. I was filled with it, soaked in it. I was having a moment with the Creator of the universe.

• • •

The second breadcrumb came in the form of a journal entry penned more than a decade before. One of the most traumatizing things for me in our whole mess was the hurtful words Micah spoke during that time. For example, one of his good friends tried to reach out to him and reminded him of how passionate he was about me when we were dating. His answer to him was that he never loved me at all! He claimed the only reason he married me was to "prove a point." He had felt in competition with a man I went to college with, who was pursuing me at the time. The only reason he married me, he said, was to "win." He called our marriage "a mistake."

That's what he called it. That's what he called me.

Marriage counselors can tell you that couples often struggle to keep the fire alive in a marriage, especially if they have young children. Parents can get so caught up in their children that they forget their spouse. Affairs tend to happen in that state, when a man loses the attention of his wife and does not have the same domestic pull she does. I assumed that's what happened to us, that Micah had the common "seven-year itch," only at ten years in. As he pointed out to me and I'd admitted to him, I *had* been too caught up in our children.

But he didn't just end it there, at that place in our marriage. He went back in time and tried to void out even the beginning of our relationship. To take everything away from me was bad enough, but to pull the rug out from everything we *ever had* was close to unbearable. He was saying that our whole happy life together was a lie. All of my fondest and loveliest memories—one-sided.

I think out of all the things he said to me at that time, that may have been the hardest thing to hear. It's one thing to believe you are not loved; it's another to believe you never were. Something deep in my heart told me these words weren't true. I believed Micah believed them, which hurt all the same, but they felt untrue nonetheless.

After receiving my next breadcrumb I knew for certain that what Micah was speaking was only lies the enemy was causing him to believe. At the time, he was barely speaking to me at all. But one day, for a reason I don't know, he asked me to find an old box that was full of things he had kept from college. While searching for the box, I found an old black journal that Micah had kept during the years we dated.

For ten years it had been hidden and undisturbed in a trunk upstairs. I had never read it before. That in itself is a miracle. I am quite nosy! But it was packed away in a closet and forgotten. Now I knew why. I was meant to read it that day. He tried to say he never loved me at all, but the journal was written by a young man very much in love.

The first entry read "For Shauna," but as I read further, I realized it was more of his prayer journal to God and for himself. He talked of the struggles of long-distance dating and how hard it was for him to be away from me. He referred to me as "the girl of his dreams" and pondered how God would even give him someone like me. He called me beautiful and said he would be a fool to ever let me go.

One entry I found particularly amusing was a list he had written of things he wanted in a wife. The very first thing on the list read, "someone who understands that love is more than a feeling."

Ha! I felt more than qualified to be his wife by that standard! I felt validated, even vindicated. Even if he didn't want me now, he wanted me once. I was exactly what he had been asking God for at one time.

The journal covered a period of two years, and in those two years he wrote of me frequently. His words were real and true and they did something to my soul as I read on. Unknown to him at the time, he had written me a love letter, allowing me to peek into his heart and mind and see where he stood at the time. He was saying *now* he never loved me. But he *did*. He was saying he didn't love me now. But I didn't believe that either.

I believe God saved this journal for me. He knew the words Micah would speak to me. He knew the hurt and damage that would be done by my hearing them. He needed me to believe in him and for me to hold on to his truth, not the lies Micah believed. The enemy (the thief) had brazenly tried to march right up into my own house and convince me that what was mine—I didn't have! That my marriage was a sham and my family was broken beyond repair. Of course, the devil's tricks only work if you believe them, and I didn't.

• • •

The third breadcrumb was a song. After reading Micah's journal, I handed it over to Micah, and I asked him to read it. I was hoping something in it would spark a passion he once had for me and remind him that as a young man he desired after God. I hoped maybe he would want that back too. He read a few pages and made a comment that it was goofy and embarrassing and put it aside.

Although I was so encouraged when I first read the journal, I only read through it once. It made my heart glad to read about all the love Micah had for me back then. But also, it made me sad for all I had lost. I wasn't quite ready to part with the journal yet, but I couldn't face the sadness it brought either. I didn't know what to do with it, so it remained open on the counter where Micah had stopped reading. I left it there and walked by it every day. Some days I pondered rereading it, but my heart hurt too badly.

One day, as I passed by the counter, the date on the open entry caught my eye: 11-04-02.

*That's odd.* I thought. *Today is November 4. Maybe I am meant to read it today?* I read the entry. It seemed insignificant. I wanted to read ahead to the next entry dated 11-05-02, but I stopped myself, thinking maybe I would need to read that tomorrow.

The next day, I woke up with the song "Deeply in Love" stuck in my head. That was odd because I hadn't listened to that song in years. I first heard it about twelve years prior, while I was away at college. I didn't know who sang it, but I remember thinking I needed to look it up so I could play it again. It was a beautiful worship song about falling in love with God, very fitting for the season of life I was in.

I headed downstairs to read the journal entry marked with the day's date. Nothing particular stuck out to me in the entry. Micah had written about my birthday coming up and how he was preparing to send me a package. He had made me a worship CD and was sending me a T-shirt that he helped design for a project he had been working on.

After reading the entry, I felt disappointed. Maybe I was hoping for too much and it was just a coincidence that the journal was opened to the day's date. I didn't know what I was searching for anyway. It's like I just wanted some miracle to jump off the page and assure me everything was going to be okay.

I tried to bury my disappointment. My two youngest sons, who were still too young for school, were home with me during the day. They of course had no idea what was going on, and I didn't want them to see their momma sad. I had to go about my usual daily tasks without allowing myself to indulge in pity parties, even when that's all I wanted to do.

Later on that same morning, I loaded the kids into the car to head to an appointment. When I got in the car, I reached for the cord I plug my phone into so I could listen to worship music on the way. As I picked it up, I realized the cord had broken. Frustration overwhelmed me. How could I focus on God and control my thoughts in silence? I needed music!

Almost frantically, I popped open the center console and started rummaging through the CDs. I grabbed one that was at the bottom. It was old and scratched and wasn't in a case. I still didn't realize what I had in my hand until my eyes caught sight of the scribbles written on it, which immediately sent goose bumps all over my body.

*"Happy Birthday, Sweetheart."*

I couldn't believe what I had in my hand. Merely an hour ago, I had read about the day Micah was making and sending me this CD over a decade before. It was created and sent to me by a man who loved me very much. Now I held it in my hands. I had no idea how it had gotten into my car, nor did I know it was there or that it even still existed. I pushed it into the player and the first song began playing perfectly. The song was "Deeply in Love."

● ● ●

All three of these breadcrumbs convinced me that God was confirming for me not only that I was to continue loving Micah, but also that my marriage was not over. They offered me hope when I otherwise had no reason to hope. God was promising me that I could hold on to that hope. I believed he would restore my husband to me.

This feeling of relief and confidence that God was making me this exciting promise was accompanied by a very sobering feeling in my soul again. God was leaving me breadcrumbs. *God.* The One who rules the Universe. The enormity of what was actually happening gave me a very reverent feeling.

In the messy reality I was living in, I had been given something I could tangibly hold on to and enjoy with my senses. I found myself once again pondering how God could be so near, so concerning, so dedicated to my wholeness.

As I drove to the appointment that day, I looked up at the sky. The trees. The expanse of the mountains that God created. I listened to my song. My song that God so calculatingly orchestrated for me to have that day. The open journal, the broken cord, having the long drive that day, which created the perfect time for me to listen to my song. The fact Micah had written that entry on the same date many years ago and that it would coincide with *that day*, of all the days.

I truly needed that gift that day. I had been feeling so desperate. I was starting to panic. Did God really see all of those things? Was God in all of those details, arranging things for me? Was he arranging things, setting them in place to encourage me even a decade before things started to unravel?

He orchestrated the events that led to these tangible breadcrumbs for me, not just once, but three times—and just in this situation alone. How many times in my life, I wondered, did he speak to me, trying to give me gifts? Help when I needed it? I wondered if he was not able to get my attention because my mind and heart were so filled with my own busyness and cares of this life.

• • •

As I set out to write this chapter, I had already decided to give it the title "Breadcrumbs." My first thought was of the children's tale *Hansel and Gretel*. I imagined the two children in the dark forest, trying to stay on the correct path. The brother and sister placed breadcrumbs on their trail so they would not forget the way they were supposed to be going. They intended to follow the breadcrumbs to remind them of the way that would lead them home to safety.

I needed to be reminded every day to stay on the correct path. It was not easy to stay in the situation I was in, deal with the hurt, and refuse to give up on my husband. The decision to stay on track using my 1 Corinthians 13 Love Filter was very intentional. It did not come naturally. It was a daily battle. So I saw these tangible breadcrumbs as reminders, signs that I was on the right track and that I was to keep going.

That was my initial thinking for the title "Breadcrumbs." However, after writing this chapter and rereading it, I thought of another story of breadcrumbs that actually happened in real life and is more fitting for this story. And our stories had some similarities.

It's the story in Exodus of the wandering Israelites. They were perpetual travelers. So that they would not go hungry in the wilderness, God sent them crumbs of bread from heaven which they called manna. They needed food to continue their physical journey, and God sent it to them daily.

Have you ever heard people make remarks like, "Why doesn't God do miracles for us now like he did in the Bible?" or "Why doesn't God send down manna from heaven these days?" Could it be that God is doing miracles, but we don't have the eyes of faith to see them? Or he does send miracles, but in our eyes they seem too small, so we complain about them, just as the Israelites complained of the manna (Num. 11:4–6)?

Thankfully, God gave me not only my own small miracles, he also gave me the eyes to see them and the heart to be grateful for them. When I was on my own desperate journey, God provided what I needed. Just what I needed. Just as miraculously.

My own desert story was that my husband betrayed me and refused to love me. God said to love him anyway. It wasn't a matter of physical life and death. Still, it was just as important for me to obey as it was for the Israelites to leave Egypt. Because God said for me to do it.

He sent what I needed. Had I truly believed that Micah never loved me and all of our years together were a lie, could I have continued in blind obedience and loved Micah anyway? I don't know. Maybe not. Had I not received the promise that Micah would be restored to me and would be my friend for all time, could I have kept going on my own journey? I can't say.

Sometimes we find ourselves up against the face of adversity and God tells us to be strong, to keep moving forward. Whether it's traveling through a dry desert or facing rejection and hurt, God sends us what we need. In my place of total dependence on God, he sent me my own manna, breadcrumbs that I needed to continue on my journey.

There are those who would chalk these experiences up to "coincidence." I'm sure we label God's provision as such more often than we should, but I know this: I received my own miracle bread from God while on my journey. I was there. I traveled this journey, and I ate bread. And I lived.

# Chapter 10

# Aaron and Hur

*When Moses' hands grew tired, they took a stone
and put it under him and he sat on it. Aaron and
Hur held his hands up—one on one side, one on the
other—so that his hands remained steady till sunset.*

EXODUS 17:12

In addition to the breadcrumbs, God also sent me an Aaron and a Hur, two spiritual stalwarts to fight beside me and hold me up when I grew weary. Who were Aaron and Hur? Their story is found in Exodus 17. The Amalekites had attacked Israel. As Joshua led the Israelites into battle, Moses, Aaron, and Hur went on top of a nearby hill. When Moses lifted up his hands, the Israelites would start winning the war. However, if Moses's arms got tired and he lowered them, the Amalekites would begin to win. So Aaron and Hur held up Moses's hands for him.

I did not tell many people of my marital troubles. Telling my family was out of the question because I knew they would jump to my rescue and it would be so very hard for them to remain objective. I do not fault them. On the contrary, I do not know many parents who would encourage their child to willingly go through heartache for someone else. In fact, I can imagine a few of my family members who, faster than anything, would have had an "escape plan" and a U-Haul parked in front of my house. I'm not sure I would do any differently if it were my daughter.

So I intentionally remained mum to certain people. At first I thought I would be going through this battle alone. My plan of action was obedience to God first. But loving Micah according to 1 Corinthians 13 was proving to be a difficult task in the face of such personal heartache. Honestly, I had never faced anything more difficult in my life.

After Micah told me he wanted out of our marriage, the first person I went to was Micah's Aunt Jan. I wanted to tell only a few people that I trusted and who I knew loved Micah as much as they loved me. He did not need people who were against him, but people who I hoped could offer him sound advice.

I also contacted Micah's older half-sister Shannon to let her know that her brother had lost his ever-lovin' mind and was trying to throw away his family. I was absolutely at the end of my rope with him and nothing I was doing seemed to be working. I thought if I was going to be replaced in the family, at least they should know.

I knew Micah had a lot of respect for both of these women, and since he wasn't listening to me, I hoped he would at least pause for a minute and listen to one of them. And if he did not, then they at least should know what was going on.

I don't really know what I expected out of Aunt Jan or Shannon when I told them. I was really just tattling on Micah to these members of his family that I knew might talk to him for me. I expected some shock at learning Micah was ending our marriage after a seemingly happy ten years, but also expected the usual response of, "let me know if you need anything." I expected to spend a few moments crying on their shoulders before the news wore off, and then I would be on my own again.

What I expected is not what I got. These two women would

soon become my close companions, my Aaron and Hur. As soon as I told them my story—what Micah had said to me and what God had said—they were on the journey with me for the long haul. They held up my arms on many occasions. I will forever be humbled by God's provision to me through them and the role they played in my battle. Any wins that were accomplished in that stage of my life and in any stage after, I credit to their obedience to God by offering their help to me.

These women took it upon themselves to check in on me often. During their own personal devotion time, God would intrude on my behalf and give them something for *me*. It seemed like my own little disaster had taken over their worlds too. They were on call for me. I could say, "I need you! Cancel your plans." They would reply, "Okay, on my way now."

But I did not need to ask for help often. I would be fighting off doubt and my phone would beep with the Scripture that I needed to fight it off. And I mean, *silently* fighting. They could not have known at that moment that I needed the encouragement. They could not have known how spot-on they were. They became true extensions of God to me in my battle.

This happened so many times that if I felt discouraged or weak in the resolve God had given me, I came to expect a correspondence or communication from one of them. This expectation came from a growing faith in God's faithfulness to me. I *knew* he would not give me more than I could bear. Instead, God gave me what I needed each step of the way.

One day I stumbled across 1 Corinthians 12:26: "If one part suffers, every part suffers with it; if one part is honored, every part rejoices with it."

I had never experienced this kind of Christian community before. More often than not, people are just too busy for each other. We feel that our own problems or agendas are reason enough not to be bothered with the problems of others. Plainly stated, we are self-absorbed and self-consumed. We are much too preoccupied to pour into another person or even make much room in our brains to think much about someone else.

That made my "Aaron and Hur's" involvement in my case all the more humbling to me. By having them to walk through that with me, I felt God's provision in an overwhelming way. It was God providing me with an extension of himself. These women were burdened for me. They took my battle *personally*. They fought with me *intensely*.

They put themselves last and gave my family top priority. Even in all of my hurt, they provided me solace. The word *solace* actually means "alleviation in distress." Imagine. We have the ability to not only walk along beside someone who is hurting, but to actually *alleviate, or lessen* their distress. Even in situations that seem to be outside of human control, we have the capability to provide solace and comfort to one another.

Although the healing itself came from God, the comfort in that time was provided to me in part through people. They provided encouragement and they were constant reminders of hope. The truth is, I don't believe I could have done this alone. Their nearness taught me several lessons.

We need each other. It is good to be burdened for one another and also to accept one another's help. Sometimes accepting that help can itself be a challenge. Some of you reading this may be thinking how nice it would have been to have someone invest in your life in the way I describe. But perhaps the truth is, you could have had that. Maybe someone was willing to walk alongside you and help carry your burdens, but pride got in the way, and you refused their help. It's difficult to admit when we can't do something alone.

I have never in my life found it easy to ask for help. I don't like exposing my weaknesses to other people, and like most humans, I like success and not failure. I have some measure of pride, and it was humiliating to admit that my husband was miserable with me and that I had failed. At this season in my life, however, my failures were unavoidable. I had hit rock bottom so I could no longer think of my pride. I couldn't care less what my situation looked like on the outside. I just wanted it fixed. Only out of my desperation was I able to accept this provision that I had never experienced before.

My Aaron and Hur were honest and truthful with me, but always hopeful. They did not coddle me when I was feeling sorry for myself. They were sensitive to my feelings but would not let me wallow in them. They were constantly encouraging me to obey God despite what was going on around me. I couldn't control what Micah was doing, they reminded me, but I could control my own reactions. By speaking God's words to me, they increased my faith and strengthened my spirit.

In that season of my life, I was wrecked. They were wrecked with me. I cried, and they cried with me. I couldn't eat, and they were sick too. They laid hands on me and prayed over me. They *believed* with me and interceded for my husband and my family. They believed me when I told them that God had told me not to give up on my husband, and they made it their business to hold me to that.

Shannon would come over and help with the kids, make them food, and put them to bed when I was too frazzled to think. She would stay up most of the night with me and then go to work the next day on two hours of sleep.

There was one night in particular I was especially distraught. After having so much hope for my marriage, Micah told me again that he wanted to be with the other woman. I was such a mess. Shannon had just gotten a new kind of braces put on that day and her mouth was swollen and she could hardly even speak. She was in a lot of pain, yet through a bleeding mouth she still stumbled through hours of conversations and counsel with me that night.

Aunt Jan came over to clean my house and, as she called it,

"alleviate triggers" that might add friction to our situation. She rubbed my back and my forehead and massaged my feet as she prayed with me. She brought me gifts, made me hot tea, and walked me through Scripture verses. I can still close my eyes and feel the calm she would bring to me.

I learned through Aunt Jan and Shannon what Christian community can be. I still feel honored even now to have shared in their friendship and to have been loved by them so selflessly. They had nothing to gain from comforting me in my darkest season, but they loved God so much, their love had turned outward. Their love for God had in turn created love and compassion for me.

I had to give them their own chapter in this book because the truth is, despite God's miraculous provisions to me, the words he spoke to me, and the breadcrumbs he sent me, in my heart I believe I would have faltered if left on my own. My arms would surely have grown weak had it not been for God providing me another miracle: my people.

Not just people, but people of God who were already seeking him, looking for ways to be used by him. I wonder how many people God has allowed to cross my path who were going through a situation and I could have helped, but I was too self-consumed to notice. I hope to always remember Aunt Jan's and Shannon's self-less natures and try to imitate them.

I knew God loved Micah very much. I felt like he was moving heaven and earth to reach him, to show his kindness to him. God could have opened up the heavens and displayed for Micah the grandest show the universe has ever seen and spelled Micah's name out in the Northern Lights to get his attention to show him that he loved him. But instead, God used his preferred method of choice. He used what he esteems even over his grand creation, what he has desired to use in every single generation that ever lived on the earth.

He chooses to use people. He uses us.

# • Chapter 11 •

# Exodus

*For everything that was written in the past was
written to teach us, so that through the endurance
taught in the Scriptures and the encouragement they
provide we might have hope.*

ROMANS 15:4

In late October I had started going to Wednesday night Bible study with Shannon at her church out of desperation. I was desperate for any words from God that might encourage my faith. And honestly, part of me just wanted to get out of the house away from the cold shoulder I was getting at home. At the very first study I attended, as soon as I took my seat in the church that evening, a verse popped up on the screen.

It was Nehemiah 4:14: "After I looked things over, I stood up and said to the nobles, the officials and the rest of the people, 'Don't be afraid of them. Remember the Lord, who is great and awesome, and fight for your families, your sons and your daughters, your wives and your homes.'" A prerecorded Beth Moore proclaimed, "I know this verse says to fight for your wives, but this is a woman's event so I'm gonna make it applicable here. Fight for your husbands!"[1]

*Okay, God, you have my attention.*

She started talking about the Ebenezer stone. A few weeks earlier I would have had no idea what that even meant. The only Ebenezer I knew of was Scrooge McDuck from an old Christmas cartoon. But thanks to All Sons & Daughters doing a cover of the old hymn, "Come Thou Fount of Every Blessing," I had the song stuck in my head. I loved the message of it and even remembered singing it as a child. Yet as I listened, I realized I didn't even know the meaning of the line that says, "Here I raise my Ebenezer, hither by thy help I come."

So I looked it up. I found the answer in 1 Samuel 7, which tells the story of the Philistines gearing up for war against Israel. As they gathered and prepared to attack, God "thundered with loud thunder against the Philistines and threw them into such a panic that they were routed before the Israelites" (v. 10). Israel then used the mass confusion of the Philistines to pursue and defeat them. Verse 12 says, "Then Samuel took a stone and set it up between Mizpah and Shen. He named it Ebenezer, saying, 'Thus far the Lord has helped us.'" For *Ebenezer* means stone of help.

I thought it an odd coincidence that Ebenezer would be the subject of the Bible study, especially after I had only recently for the first time learned about the meaning of that name. I figured there was something in it God wanted to speak to me. I was learning that most "coincidences" in this season were not coincidences at all—but rather God orchestrating something. In the days and weeks to come, this Scripture would become monumental in my own journey.

The study continued on. The children of Israel had been wandering the desert for nearly forty years. They had been slaves in Egypt until God sent Moses to rescue them. Most of us know the story about all the wonders and miracles God did for them in their Exodus journey during their wanderings. Joshua 3 and 4 finds the Israelites under the command of Joshua. It had been a long and tiresome journey and they had just reached the Jordan River.

The Message translation explains what happened:

> The people left their tents to cross the Jordan, led by the priests carrying the Chest of the Covenant. When the priests got to the Jordan and their feet touched the water at the edge (the Jordan overflows its banks throughout the harvest), the flow of water stopped. It piled up in a heap—a long way off—at Adam, which is near Zarethan. The river went dry all the way down to the Arabah Sea (the Salt Sea). And the people crossed, facing Jericho. And there they stood; those priests carrying the Chest of the Covenant stood firmly planted on dry ground in the middle of the Jordan while all Israel crossed on dry ground. Finally the whole nation was across the Jordan, and not one wet foot.
>
> JOSHUA 3:14–17

For the second time in the Israelites' exodus, God parted waters for this nation. The story continues as God instructs Joshua to command twelve men, one from each tribe, to go and gather twelve stones from the middle of the Jordan and carry them into the camp where they would stay the night. The passage continues, "Cross to the middle of the Jordan and take your place in front of the Chest of GOD, your God. Each of you heft a stone to your shoulder, a stone for each of the tribes of the People of Israel, so you'll have something later to mark the occasion. When your children ask you, 'What are these stones to you?' you'll say, 'The flow of the Jordan was stopped in front of the Chest of the Covenant of God as it crossed the Jordan—stopped in its tracks. These stones are a permanent memorial for the People of Israel'" (Josh. 4:4–7 MSG).

What was notable to me was that God commanded they set up the stones at the camp where they were staying that night, not at their destination. Beth Moore put it so eloquently, but I will try and paraphrase what she said. They were not in Egypt (where they were slaves in bondage) anymore, but they were not in Canaan (the Promised Land) yet either. She called this the "Place of Crisis."

*Aha!* When she put it like that, I understood the relationship of this story to me. I was in crisis too. They were in an Exodus, *the waiting.* I am not putting my own sufferings on par with the Israelites who wandered in the desert and survived off of manna for forty years as they waited for their promised land. But I did relate to this story, now more than ever. I had left "Egypt" and I couldn't go back even if I wanted to. I had not arrived or received my promise yet. But God wanted to set up memorials of all the things he had done here in the waiting, a testimony of his provision along the way. The journey—before the arrival—was very significant. That was the Israelites' testimony. That is my testimony.

I started setting up stones. My daily battle was a struggle. I was 1 Corinthians 13-ing the pudding out of Micah, mostly to have it backfire in my face and inflict more damage on myself. I kept hearing God speak of promises yet to come, for not only a renewed relationship—but to bring Micah back to himself. I wasn't even exactly sure what all I was holding on for, to be honest. I just heard God saying to hold on, so I was doing my best.

When Joshua set up the stones at camp, it was to be a sign. They had not even arrived at their destination, but the stones were a monument declaring, "This far, God has helped us." I knew God had started something. I knew I hadn't arrived yet, but here in the waiting, God was with me. For the Israelites, no, they were not physically in Canaan yet, but *my goodness,* God just parted the waters for them! That is something. *"This far,* God has helped us."

I started counting wins. After all that had happened, I did not want to give up and I did not feel like a complete mess like I knew I should have been. God had been strengthening me. Win. Lay a stone down. *This far, God has helped me.* Weeks ago, Micah had said he was leaving the house, but he had stayed thus far. Win. Lay a stone down. God had sent me breadcrumbs. Win. Lay a stone down. God would speak an encouraging word to me in my quiet time. I laid down a stone and declared, *"This far, God has helped me."*

In case you are wondering, no, I did not lay real actual stones all over my house. If I had, my kids would've busted out every single window in the house for sure! But I would stop and thank God and realize his help to me on this journey. I knew he was helping me in my situation or I would not have been able to come so far.

I loved how Beth Moore explained that Scripture too. I won't quote her directly, but she explained it something like this: Sometimes we can't make it through the day. We are so weary from our journey that we can't take one more step. At that moment we have to come to Jesus for help and cry, "God, I am stuck. You are gonna have to part some waters if you want me to keep going!"

In my case, I was able to find renewal by reading his Word, worshiping, or simply crying out to him. Once a day wasn't enough. I did those things every hour, several times a day, or as often as I needed. I was "in the trenches" of my fight, and sometimes I had to take it hour by hour. Pretty soon weeks had gone by and I could see that I was still journeying, and had not given up! The farther along you journey, the less you find you want to give up and turn back around. *This far, God has helped me.*

I shared about the Ebenezer stone with Micah one night. It was a rare moment when he had let his guard down to me. We were lying in bed facing each other. The light was dim. He said, "I don't know where your confidence is coming from. I don't know how you can even stand being in the same room with me, let alone trying to fight for me. I don't understand why you want to be with me, not even knowing if I am going to stay with you or not, or whether I will be here tomorrow."

I smiled at him like I had a little secret. I explained about the Ebenezer stone and responded, "I don't know about tomorrow. But I know that this far, up until right now, God has helped me." Beth

Moore said in her study, "I don't know about tomorrow, but today God and I are making it just fine!"

I had no idea where Micah's mind was that night. But I was deliriously happy. A few short weeks ago, he was preparing to leave. His clothes were actually still packed and beside the bed as we talked. He had been cold and distant. No. Not distant. *Cut off.* He would not even make eye contact with me and flinched when I tried to embrace him. He would snap at me when I spoke, otherwise there was no communication at all. I had thought it was too late. I had thought he was gone. I had lost him. I thought I would never get to hold him, laugh with him, or ever be wanted by him again.

That night, however, I could see glimpses of a softening heart. I could see eyes that wanted to cave in and give in to being loved and accepting grace. He had such a hard heart, but that night, here we were talking about God and hope and of God's faithfulness. To an innocent onlooker it may have seemed to be just a simple conversation. To me, it was God parting the waters, bringing me safe and dry to the other side, defeating a whole army on my behalf. I saw God's hand in it. And I named it Ebenezer. *This far, God has helped me.*

And I knew in the morning he would help me again.

• • •

I continued going to Wednesday night Bible study with Shannon. The next week, a prerecorded but oh-so-relevant and on-time for me, Beth Moore continued to lead me on a journey. She set the scene of the battle in Joshua, the same battle where the sun stood still in the sky. The people of God were completely surrounded. They trudged all night long, carrying their heavy armor and weaponry, and were set to fight an uphill battle. They must have been exhausted and aggravated. They did not instigate this battle, yet here they trudged, dragged into a battle they did not want to fight. Surely they felt they were marching to their deaths. *But where Satan plans the perfect setup for defeat, God provides the perfect stage to show off!*

He did it in the battle against the Amorites, and he did it in the desert for the Israelites. He *showed off*. He knew there was certain death and defeat if he didn't move. And so did the Israelites. I can almost see God cracking his knuckles, "This is some of my best work. Sit back and enjoy!"

One day after what I thought had been a few "good days," Micah caught me off guard and admitted he was still thinking of this other person "a lot lately" and that he still wanted to be with her. That evening, I felt frustrated and called Kim, a dear friend of mine, and I vented. I didn't doubt what God told me to do. I knew he told me to love Micah according to his Word, to not give up, to fight for Micah, and to endure and to hope. I got all that, loud and clear. Not the problem.

My problem was Micah's response. I vividly remember saying to Kim, "I don't doubt *what* God is telling me to do. I don't understand *why* he is telling me to do it! Every time I react in love toward Micah, he pushes me away even more. It's having the opposite effect of what I want! Why would God have me do this?"

She told me not to think of everything I was doing as just a sacrifice of love to Micah. Ultimately, God was the one who had given me clear words to follow. So when it gets hard and Micah's actions disappoint me and do not give me the outcome or satisfaction I hoped for, I shouldn't look at it as something I am doing for him. She encouraged me to do it as a sacrifice of love unto God. It is all for him. He said to do it. My job is to obey. The end.

I remember setting my phone down on the table and thinking that I just needed to stop thinking about it. It was constantly on my mind, and I just wanted to shut 'er down for a bit. I grabbed a book off the shelf and hopped into the bath. Aunt Jan had given me the book *Wonderstruck* by Margaret Feinberg a few weeks before. I had already started it, so I found my place where I had left off.

The following is what I read:

> God instructs Moses to demand that Pharaoh, the ruler
> of Egypt, set the Israelites free. Moses obeys but becomes
> disappointed and disillusioned at the response. Instead
> of granting liberation, Pharaoh doubles the workload.
> Moses bombards God with a series of why questions:
> "Oh, Lord, why have you brought harm to this people?
> Why did you ever send me?" Instead of answering Moses'
> questions of why, God responds to Moses' questions
> with who. Just as God revealed himself in increasing
> measure to Abraham, Isaac, and Jacob, God promises to
> reveal himself to Moses and the Israelites. He fulfills the
> commitment with spectacular fanfare. Water becomes
> blood. Insects multiply. Clouds thunder. Hail descends.
> Darkness falls. The Red Sea splits. Manna appears. Water
> pours from a rock. And that's only the beginning. [2]

I immediately called Kim back (in tears this time), "God spoke to
me! I just said the same words to you that Moses said to God: Why
have me do this? *Why?* It just made it worse!" I explained that God had
responded to his questions of *why* with a *who*. God revealed himself
to Pharaoh and all the people by revealing who he was. Irrefutably.
*That's* what I knew Micah needed. And all that he needed. For God
to reveal himself. Irrefutably. Unarguably. In his heart. When God
reveals himself to you, how can you not follow him?

God reminded me once again that he wanted Micah's heart
and my obedience. For his reasons, not mine. He was capable of
accomplishing anything he wanted, anything he spoke. He is the
same God that revealed himself to Pharaoh and the Israelites, after
all. I thought, *I think he's got this.*

I was in this predicament. This place of waiting. My exodus. I'd
lost my sweetheart and was waiting on God's promise to bring him
back. My future, the future of my family and our sweet little boys

hung in a very delicate balance. The uncertainty for me was draining. But I believed the God of the Universe, of Abraham, Isaac, and Jacob, would come to my aid and not abandon me.

If anyone has ever been in a place of waiting and was excited about it, I've never met them. Not if they're being honest about it. Come on! The waiting stinks. If we could travel back in time and interview the Israelites about how they were enjoying themselves wandering around the desert, I'm sure some of them would have flipped us the bird. After all, God's patience grew thin throughout the years because the Israelites complained *so much!* The waiting, folks, is not fun.

But in my waiting, this was my manna that sustained me: His presence so *tangible*, so real, so *present* with me. Teaching me to trust him. *To really trust in him.* Learning to hear him. *I can hear him!* Falling in love with him again, being completely dependent on him. And even to say, "God, you know this outcome and I do not. Let me find my joy and purpose in you, here in the waiting. No matter the outcome." Proclaiming to God that he was all I needed and realizing for myself it was true.

I couldn't trade that in. I couldn't say, "Let's go back to before October 14 and make it all go away. Let me not hurt anymore and give me my old life back." I wouldn't say that. No way. Because in that waiting place, I had met with God. *Did you hear me?* I have met the Eternal One.

This might sound crazy, but it's been a holy adventure. I am forever changed. I am humbled that God trusted me with this opportunity to turn to him. And I think he takes pleasure in showing himself faithful to me. Even now, I realize I would rather return to a valley or a waiting place to be near him than to be on the highest mountaintop of victory without him.

Throughout this whole ordeal, the story of Exodus gave me strength. One day I read Romans 15:4 and understood why. "For everything that was written in the past was written to teach us, so that through the endurance taught in the Scriptures and the encouragement they provide we might have hope."

These Scriptures gave me *immeasurable* hope. Reading about the Israelites' Exodus and how they didn't give up even though they got tired, encouraged me. Most of all, seeing God remain faithful to them through their journey gave me hope. He is the same after all. Faithful then. Faithful now.

Again from the book *Wonderstruck*, Margaret Feinberg continues the story of the Israelites' Exodus. "Sporting chapped lips and sunburnt noses, the people of God discover the nature of God with each passing mile."[3]

I was in my own Exodus to be sure. You could see the signs of it in the waiting. The painstaking days of slow and steady progress. My chapped lips were tempting me to succumb to defeat. *I've been tossed aside. My husband has moved on without me.*

My own thoughts were my obstacles. *What are you doing? What are you waiting on? Why are you doing this to yourself? People are going to think you are pathetic. Have some dignity and move on!* Those stupid flying gnats around my head were driving me crazy! The daily battle was constant! My sunburnt nose was a heart, raw and hurting. But I was being fed manna, was walking all day, and my clothes weren't wearing out. I was sustained by a miraculous power and provision. I wasn't going to give up. And I discovered the nature of God with each passing mile.

A Scripture that moves me even now when I read it is found in Deuteronomy 8:3 AMPC: "And he humbled you and allowed you to hunger and fed you with manna, which you did not know nor did your fathers know, that he might make you recognize and personally know that man does not live by bread only, but man lives by every word that proceeds out of the mouth of the Lord."

I read this and started crying. I was sitting beside a friend, so I read it out loud as if a lightbulb had flashed on. I explained, "By the grace of God, he has allowed me to experience this 'hunger'—this need to depend on him, so that he could feed me with his supernatural food! So that I would know in my heart his goodness and his capability to provide for me." My friend shot me a raised eyebrow look, trying to determine if I was okay or not.

It's really hard to explain if you are not the one in the place of waiting—an Exodus. It's hard to imagine if you are not the starving Israelite, with sand burning your eyeballs and God provides you fresh water out of a stone. Or if you are not the discarded wife pleading with God for her husband's soul and his heart returned to her. If you are not in that desperate state, where if God doesn't move all is lost, then you can't get it. It's not your fault. You may raise your eyebrows.

But God humbled me. I had been brought low. I had been put through the ringer. The little world I lived in before had been shattered, and my family hung in a place of uncertainty. I was overwhelmed, and I fell on my knees and cried out to God in desperation. In return, he fed me with manna that I truly did not know existed. A supernatural provision of strength.

Honestly, I never would have thought God really could sustain me through something like this. (I sincerely hate to admit that, but it is still true.) To get a divorce and move on to a new relationship? Maybe. Maybe he could see me through that. That seems like it would be easier. But to hang on like a madwoman to this train wreck of a marriage, and push past the humiliation and rejection and my pride? That's a lot harder. I didn't know God would make a way for that one.

It's one thing to read about the Israelites' Exodus in the Bible. God parted the sea for them. That's awesome. He sent water forth from a rock for them. Wonderful. He provided miracle food. Yup. That's my God! But trusting that. For my own life. For real. In 2013. When my husband wanted to move on to someone else but God said, "Nope. That's not my promise for you. Hold onto him. Hope. Endure. Love. Draw close to me in the waiting." That seemed like a tall order.

# Chapter 12

# The Power of Words

*Words kill, words give life;*
*they're either poison or fruit—you choose.*
PROVERBS 18:21 MSG

Early on, I shared with Aunt Jan about the Love Filter and how God had instructed me to use 1 Corinthians 13 as a guide for my words and responses to Micah's actions. One morning, she came over with a care package. She sat her canvas tote onto the wooden floor and pulled out a tube of lip gloss. "Put this on when you have a hard time speaking to Micah in a way that reflects First Corinthians Thirteen," she said matter of factly. "It will serve as a physical reminder of what you should allow to come out of your mouth." She added, "If Micah says something you don't like and you feel a rise of anger, stop what you are doing, walk away, and apply the lip gloss."

It might sound silly, but it worked. Why? I discovered that sometimes you really have to plan ahead of time to be nice! You have to be intentional about not snapping back at someone when you know you will want to do so! On the opposite side of that, I realized that the lip gloss could also serve as a reminder of what *should* come out of my mouth: prayers and praises to God. What a help this was to me! This simple token of thoughtfulness (stroke of genius) on Aunt Jan's part helped me greatly in my quest for obedience.

I remember specific moments when I was so frustrated and angered by Micah and had an urge to retaliate. At those times, I would go get my lip gloss and apply it silently and think back through the Love Filter in my mind. It was a form of discipline for me. Like going on a daily run to train for a marathon, or watching my diet to lose weight, I had to discipline my body consistently even when I didn't feel like it. If I was to choose obedience to God, I had to *consistently and intentionally choose* obedience. I had to *plan* and *train* myself to obey.

I felt like God had called me to intercede for Micah in prayer and to mostly keep quiet. When I met with Shannon, often she would ask me what God was saying to me and if I was obeying. For a while, every time she asked, I answered her, "Yes, I do feel like God spoke to me and his instructions to me were, 'Shhhhh!'"

God wanted me to be quiet and let him do his work in peace. I was learning that just one word from the Father can accomplish more than thousands of books written by earth's most notable scholars. Micah and I have since joked about this book project. God must have given this little project to me to keep me occupied and quiet while God worked because *look at all the words!* I could have helped God so much with my insight and wisdom! Yet he said for me to stay quiet. As a human with so many words, that was a challenging task.

God had called me to show extreme discipline with my words and with this Love Filter thing. And in the course of training my tongue, I learned a very difficult lesson about the power of words to kill and destroy.

James 3:5–10 explains the power of words in a very visceral, physical way, by talking of our tongue:

> The tongue is a small part of the body, but it makes great boasts. Consider what a great forest is set on fire by a small spark. The tongue also is a fire, a world of evil among the parts of the body. It corrupts the whole body, sets the whole course of one's life on fire, and is itself set on fire by hell. All kinds of animals, birds, reptiles and sea creatures are being tamed and have been tamed by mankind, but no human being can tame the tongue. It is a restless evil, full of deadly poison. With the tongue we praise our Lord and Father, and with it we curse human beings, who have been made in God's likeness. Out of the same mouth come praise and cursing. My brothers and sisters, this should not be.

When Micah first approached me in mid-October with a petition for a divorce, he thought I would be in agreement with it. He thought the feelings (or lack thereof) were mutual. He sincerely thought that deep down, this is what I wanted. He was genuinely taken aback when I reacted the way I did. In exasperation, one day he brought up something I had spouted off nearly eight years earlier, "Remember, you said you wished I would just leave you while you were still young enough to find someone else."

What a hard way to learn the power of my words! I do not remember saying that to Micah all of those years ago, but I do remember feeling that way. The first few years of our marriage were difficult. We had lived in California for a short time at the beginning of our marriage and when we moved back to Ohio, Micah had difficulty finding work, so we moved in with my parents for a spell while he looked for something. I was pregnant with our first child, and it felt degrading and embarrassing to be living back home with my parents.

I felt like Micah had lost a bit of himself when things did not work out with his job in California and we moved back to our

home state. He ended up taking jobs he hated. At the time I felt that
he was too immature to be married and that I was not a priority to
him. I'm guessing also that in my frustrations, I quite likely was no
walk in the park either. He was unhappy and I was disappointed.

But things did not stay that way forever. Eventually, we got
back on our own two feet. Micah went back to school, and he found
employment in a career he enjoyed. We had two more beautiful
kids. Those cloudy years at the beginning of our marriage turned
into better and happier times. I would even say that at the time of
Micah's unwelcome announcement, I had never been in a happier
place in our marriage.

But our words, unlike our circumstances that change, once
spoken, do not change. They don't disappear, and it is difficult to
take them back. I had no idea the imprint my careless words had
left on my husband's soul. That seed I planted in Micah with my
spoken words got buried in his heart and festered and slowly grew
into poison. My words were hasty and thoughtless, and I had forgotten I even said them. I surely didn't feel that way now. Yet I was
paying dearly for that statement spoken carelessly years ago. That
was a lesson I had to learn.

I realized then that I had failed as a wife. For my husband to
believe that I thought so little of him that I could easily replace
him! For him not to know that I would be completely devastated by
his absence. For him not to know that I depended on him. For him
*not to know* that he was half of me and without him I was just one
half of myself—the rest an open mess, gaping and incomplete. *How
could he not know that?* I had been charged with loving this man,
and I had not. That was my failure.

I looked at this whole present mess as an opportunity to show
him how much I did love him. In the course of our marriage, I had
failed. I felt sick that he thought he could leave our family with
little reaction from me. I had to fix this. I had to show him.

I began sharing my devotions with Micah for the first time in our marriage, and allowing the Holy Spirit to lead me in the things I said. For example, one day I stumbled across Romans 8:20–21, "The creation was subjected to frustration, not by its own choice, but by the will of the one who subjected it, in hope that the creation itself will be liberated from its bondage to decay and brought into the freedom and glory of the children of God."

When I read that, I immediately thought of Micah's frustration with our mediocre Christian life. He was so fed up, in fact, he was willing to risk everything to find something more. This Scripture passage makes it sound like that frustration was *created in us* and was *on purpose!* We are not supposed to feel or be complete unless completed by the Creator.

I shared this passage, along with my epiphany, with Micah. I said, "Yes, you went about filling that void the wrong way. But at least you felt it!" It was good he became miserable. It led me to my spiritual renaissance. I was so content with our mediocre, complacent life I probably would never have moved forward toward God without this catastrophe. So I thanked Micah for the catastrophe! I affirmed him for calling us out, and at least being aware that something was wrong!

Studying the Exodus story has changed the way I read God's Word. Before, when I read the Bible it seemed so very personal that I kept my thoughts to myself. Then I ran across this passage that has taught me to be outward and vocal about the things I read and learn in his Word. Deuteronomy 6:6–9 talks about the importance of speaking God's word plainly, openly, and often: "These commandments that I give you today are to be on your hearts. Impress them on your children. Talk about them when you sit at home and when you walk along the road, when you lie down and when you get up. Tie them as symbols on your hands and bind them on your foreheads. Write them on the doorframes of your houses and on your gates."

So I began to do this (minus the tying them to my forehead

part). I talked about God's Word openly to Micah, to the kids, to my friends, just as I would talk to them about anything else. It was awkward at first. I ignored the awkwardness and did it anyway until it became natural. It became a part of living—a more empowered way of living. There is power in God's words.

Maybe it's hard for us to comprehend the kind of power in God's Word because our own words mean so little. The concept that there is power in words becomes distorted to humans because we base our trust in words based on our experiences with people. Our words mean very little. We break our promises all the time. We make promises we can't keep, or won't keep, or just lie right from the beginning, having no intention of keeping our word at all.

Even simple mistakes that are not malicious teach us to devalue our words. For example, I tell my child I am going to go to the store to get him milk while he's in school so that after school he can have milk and cookies. He comes home excited, expecting to have such a nice treat. But when he opens the fridge he is sorely disappointed.

"Oh, shoot. I forgot to get your milk. Sorry."

God does not do that! *We do that.* We are unreliable, he's not. We can't base our opinions of God's promises on what we have learned from each other while living here on this earth. We have to base our opinions on what he himself says in his Word. He is always faithful and true and he does what he says he'll do.

So, I stuck with speaking the only things I was sure of: God's Word. I brought it into everyday practical conversations. Even when I didn't know where Micah's heart was, God's Word never returns void! Isaiah 55:11 says, "So is my word that goes out from my mouth: It will not return to me empty, but will accomplish what I desire and achieve the purpose for which I sent it." God's Word accomplishes what he desires.

Thank God it is not dependent on the reliability of the one who reads and speaks it. As you will soon see, I was about to become pretty unreliable.

# Chapter 13

# "It's Over"

*Finally, brothers and sisters, whatever is true,*
*whatever is noble, whatever is right, whatever is pure,*
*whatever is lovely, whatever is admirable—if anything*
*is excellent or praiseworthy—think about such things.*
PHILIPPIANS 4:8

In mid-November, I woke up with a Bible verse in my head. Not just in my head—it was *hovering over me*. I heard it clearly, replaying softly in my mind. My youngest son, Judah, had woken up crying in the night, so I had gotten into bed with him and when I woke up that morning, I was still in his bottom bunk. I remember opening my eyes and staring at the blue metal bars over my head that supported the top bunk as I heard this verse pound over and over in my head: "Whatever is true, whatever is noble, whatever is right, whatever is pure, whatever is lovely . . . think about such things."

But I was conflicted that morning. I had discovered the name of the woman with whom my husband had an affair. We had mutual friends on social media. It would be all too easy to find out who she was and what she looked like. I felt eerily calm.

I wanted the mystery of it to end and was hoping (however absurdly) to find some closure, some resolve. It still didn't really feel like Micah was working with me on our relationship, but at this point he was at least *saying* he was going to try to make things work with me. He at least said the relationship with the other woman was over.

So what could it hurt to look her up? I just wanted to be able to go into a store without looking around at every woman who was close to our age wondering if she had slept with my husband. I thought the enemy I knew would be better than the enemy I didn't. My reasoning was absurd, of course, but in my brokenness at that time, it made sense.

*Whatever is true, whatever is noble, whatever is right, whatever is pure, whatever is lovely. . . . think about such things.* I heard this ringing loudly as I lay in my son's bed. It was as if I could see a spiritual fork in the road as I lay there pondering my dilemma. I knew deep down that investigating this woman could not lead to any of those things in the verse. I knew deep down that even though I desperately wanted closure, this was not going to be my quick fix. It could not possibly take my mind to a good place.

But I remember making a decision and thinking, *My husband cheated on me. I deserve at least to know with whom.* I even rationalized that I had been more than kind in this situation, and I would not give up this one small thing. I *demanded* at that moment to know who she was. I chose to go left when I knew to go right.

It's crazy how vividly I remember that decision. Even if my reasoning had been correct, which it wasn't, my decision was clearly in conflict with the verse God had placed on my heart that morning. I let go of Jesus' hand that had been leading and guiding me, *sheltering* me. I dropped it to go chase a rabbit. He spoke direction to me and I chose to go against it. How could that possibly be a good thing to think about since I was trying to work on things with my husband? Our marriage was in a very delicate place. Micah was trying to do the right thing, but not feeling anything.

There was no way that decision could have been beneficial, as I found out later when I explained to Shannon what I had done. She looked at me like I had an alien sitting on my head and advised me to run my harebrained ideas by her next time. But I had wanted to do it and had convinced myself it was okay, even though I knew it was wrong.

I'll spare you the gory details of the day and just give you the CliffsNotes version. I have a friend who had been cheated on in a previous relationship, so I knew she would understand what I was going through. I noticed that on social media, she was a mutual friend of the mystery woman. I didn't tell her who the woman was, but I did ask her to allow me to use her password and username so I could effectively hack into this woman's private page and see her pictures. Good, solid plan, right? Suuuure.

"She" was the most beautiful thing I had ever seen. Or at least that's what my brain told me when I looked at her in that moment. I felt like if given the chance to choose my own appearance, it would be exactly hers. She had the hair that I have always wanted. Even as a little girl I dreamed of having her soft, blond curly hair. Her face was beautiful, adorable. She looked fit, trim, and trendy. In that moment, I realized my worst nightmare had come true. I was hoping she would have obvious flaws or at least something I could find that I could convince myself was a flaw. I was hoping I could look at her and feel like I stood a chance against her, but this dissolved that fantasy.

My heart died immediately. It sank fast, all the way to my feet, making my stomach sick as it passed down. *At once* my brain began painting all the images of the love affair. Up until that moment, I had been shielded, my thoughts carefully guarded. But the eyes are the window to the soul, and in that moment I lost control. I couldn't get the images out of my mind—*her with my husband*. No. *No!* I couldn't do this. It was too much to ask. I *hate* her. I *hate* him.

I was done. Even if Micah's heart really had been for me at this point, which it wasn't, I could never let him touch me again. I knew it. I could not compare to that. I knew it. Even if we reconciled, I would always wonder in the back of my mind if he was imagining her, wishing I was better. I would never be enough.

I could feel the meltdown coming quickly as all my hope drained out of me. I had to hide myself from the kids, so I left Micah at the house with the kids and took off walking. I didn't know where I was going, so I grabbed my credit card and phone just in case. I had no plan. I just needed to walk and be alone—and lose it. Up until that moment, I had maintained my composure. I had been in my God bubble. Now, however, I was allowing myself to go crazy, and crazy I went.

It was dark already, raining and cold. It also happened to be Wednesday, the day I was supposed to go to Bible study with Shannon. When she came to pick me up that evening, I was not there. I didn't answer my phone. I was done. *It's over.*

As I trudged along in the rain, I despaired. Blinded by the darkness and my tears, I wound my way down an unkempt street with unruly hedges that smacked my arm and soaked my shoulder as I passed by. A dog barked and banged against a crooked metal fence, pushing me into a puddle. The smell of a nearby Papa John's, which I would normally love, now turned my stomach sour. I stumbled over jagged chunks of cracked sidewalks while the cold rain pounded my head.

I had wanted to hold my husband, to feel him embrace me and to have him back. I had so much hope before! But I knew I could never have him back now. I was heartbroken. I would never be able to accept any kind of affection from him again. This hurt too much; our relationship was beyond repair.

*How could he do this to me? How could he hurt me so badly?* I was even angry that everyone around him was showing him so much love and support. *I am the one hurting here! Got that? Me! He caused this!* I sulked. I had wanted to take him back, but I knew now that I couldn't. It would never be the same. I would always wonder in the back of my mind. . . . *Oh, the questions with which I would torment myself!* I just couldn't do it. I quickly spiraled into despair.

By that time, Aunt Jan and Shannon were calling and texting me from my porch. I ignored them. When I finally answered my phone, I was belligerent. "I know what you are going to say already! That I am backing down on my word. That I am giving up, that I am not listening to God. Well, I am done. Everyone is so focused on Micah *and loving Micah* and I am so over it! I have been hurt beyond repair here! Do you hear me? I can't do this. It's over. I hate it, but it's over." I will never forget Aunt Jan. She responded sweetly and firmly, "I just want to know where you are so I can go with you." With that, I grew ashamed of myself. I knew I was out of line. God had provided me a bubble and I refused to stay with him. He had given me a way to be protected in all of this and I turned my nose up at him.

Thank God for his faithfulness that Aunt Jan and Shannon were waiting for me on my porch that night. When I finally trudged up my front steps, these two agents of God were yet again another provision. The state they found me in was a far cry from the resolve I had to fix our marriage the last time they'd left me and from the bubble they had seen me operating in the weeks before.

That night, I was rain-soaked from head to toe, wet hair matted to my head, black mascara dripping from my swollen eyes. Somewhere during my rant, the credit card had fallen out of my pocket and was lost. I had missed the Bible study. I had decided my marriage was over. I was absolutely heartbroken and had to relive the agony of that first day all over again. I was sore from shivering. I was defeated.

When I went back inside the house, Shannon had already put the kids to bed. I found Micah as expected. If he had at any point started to come out of his shell toward me, he was once again a full-grown turtle. When I had left the house, I had yelled at him and slammed the door in his face; that was it for him. That's what he had been waiting on, *his proof* that this marriage could not be fixed. The only thing attractive about me to him at that time was my God bubble. When I left it, he could not hide his disgust for me anymore. He talked to Shannon that night about the other woman and his plans to move forward with her.

Aunt Jan, being Aunt Jan, had gone into the kitchen and found some crackers and juice. She sat us both on the couch and forced us to say one thing nice about each other. Micah sat there blank-eyed and could not think of one nice thing to say. When it was my turn to talk, instead of English words, unintelligible sobs came out. Then she said, "If there is anyone in this room who loves each other, we are going to take communion!"

After the *worst communion ever*, Micah left for work. He thought we were all nuts. I just wanted to sink to the floor and die. Aunt Jan had me lie on the couch and massaged my forehead and my feet. They let me cry and listened to my sob story. I felt so sorry for myself. They tried to realign my thoughts by reminding me that God was still at work, and they fed me Scripture verses. *My job was only to be obedient. Everything else was God's job.*

They were not against me. They were not coercing me to stay with Micah. They had simply listened to me about the resolve God had given me and then encouraged me to listen to him. They were encouraging me in this quest for the impossible, because they knew God. And they knew that if he speaks, it's best to listen to him, every time, no matter what. And then follow.

"Whatever is true, whatever is noble, whatever is right, whatever is pure, whatever is lovely. . . . think about such things." Hmmm. It's almost as if God knew what he was talking about that morning when he kept pestering me with that verse! He had simply been trying to help me avoid this whole fiasco.

Shannon and Aunt Jan were able to convince me that even though I was rattled and felt like I had destroyed everything I had been working so hard for, God was not rattled. God knew I was going to make that decision before I made it. He was not on the edge of his seat, anxious that an insecure girl from Ohio had power enough to mess up his great master plan. He had his own plans, as I was soon to discover.

# Chapter 14

# New Mercies

*Because of the LORD's great love we are not*
*consumed,*
*for his compassions never fail.*
*They are new every morning;*
*great is your faithfulness.*

LAMENTATIONS 3:22–23

Aunt Jan and Shannon stayed with me that whole awful night. It was like a morgue in my living room. You would have thought someone died, for all the sadness. Around 4:30 a.m. Judah woke up crying, as he frequently did. I went upstairs to put him back to bed, but too exhausted to do anything else, I climbed into his bed and held him. After that excruciating long night, I finally fell asleep. Guess what I found in the morning?

New mercies.

New, sweet mercies. Gone were all of those things I was yammering pitifully about in the rain the night before: *I can't do this. I can never let him touch me again. I will never get over this.* Those sick feelings of despair, hopelessness, and anger—they were gone.

And I don't mean *sort of* gone. I woke up with a song in my heart and a new resolve. I awoke with joy. Not a happiness that is defined by circumstances, but *joy*—a calmness and fulfillment that can only come as a product of the working of God's wonderful supernatural presence. I wasn't defeated. I had felt defeated during the night. But I didn't feel that way in the morning. And that ugly sense of despair never returned. Still as I type this, it hasn't returned.

I knew in my heart that it didn't make sense for me to wake up with a resolve to forgive and love my husband. I was filled with a pure love for him and a determination to make up to him what I had done the night before! That peace was *beyond understanding.* There was no way I could have found that resolve and peace on my own, no matter how much determination I had.

The night before I had wanted to lay out in the cold and the rain and die. That was my grand plan, actually. That's the best I had. God said, "*No.* Come to me and there is life. I will show you fulfillment not based on your circumstances, but by my presence."

*Yes, please.*

The only way I can think to describe this phenomenon of the new mercies that met me in the morning is like a physical healing. Like when Jesus himself laid his hands on a cripple, a leper, or a blind man as described in the New Testament and they were healed. If someone would have asked them for a five steps to healing program, what would they say? What could they say? Jesus touched them and they were healed. I myself can only say, I don't know. Jesus healed me.

I was eager to start afresh in new obedience following the Love Filter. As I trusted God and saw his faithfulness and power working in my heart, my faith was increased. I knew it was not reasonable for me to be able to wake up and desire my husband after what happened the night before. It was not reasonable to awaken with such a fierce dedication to forgetting the past. It was not reasonable to wake up to a fresh confidence I didn't have just hours ago, to have hope restored in my heart again.

In reality, my reaction that night after learning the woman's identity was probably a very basic, normal, human reaction to that situation. A human instinct is to guard ourselves from pain. That's why I became defensive and hard, to protect myself from that pain again. Human tendency is to close up when hurt, and to lash out. But God's hand was over me, protecting me from my humanness to save my marriage for his bigger purpose and strengthening me to follow his commands to love my husband.

God also used that night of disaster as a teachable moment. What did I learn from this? What would I change? What would I do next time? I decided I would heed God's Word. "Whatever is true, whatever is noble, whatever is right, whatever is pure, whatever is lovely. . . . think about such things." I have found that I am safe in obedience.

Another Scripture I've known my whole life that became real to me in that season of learning is this one: "The peace of God, which transcends all understanding, will guard your hearts and your minds in Christ Jesus" (Phil. 4:7). Since I had walked out of his peace by my own choosing, I could see exactly how much peace I had been operating in before. Without God's peace, I would have gone crazy. I got a taste of "reality" apart from him. No thanks. Not for me. I would remember that night and the feeling of despair that hung on my shoulders when faced with other temptations to let my guard down, dismiss Scripture, and not take control of my thoughts.

I love this same verse in the Amplified Version. "And God's peace . . . which transcends all understanding shall garrison *and* mount guard over your hearts and minds in Christ Jesus."

These are war terms. *Garrison* means, "a body of troops stationed in a fortified place."[1] *Guard* means, "to keep safe from harm or danger; protect; watch over; to keep under close watch; to keep under control or restraint as a matter of caution."[2] This verse to me defined the bubble I had been experiencing every day. Now that I had walked outside of it, I would guard my thoughts more carefully.

What do I mean by controlling my thoughts? I decided I could not think about the affair, imagine any of the details around it, interrogate Micah about it, or try to learn anything about the mystery woman. I was not ready for it. I decided until I could think about it without feeling emotions of destruction on myself (insecurity, jealousy, fear, bitterness, anger, etc.) then I ought not think or imagine anything about it at all. I told myself that further down the road, when I had healed more, I would get my answers.

But I can tell you now, even as I heal, the affair doesn't even seem important anymore. I don't care about any of the details, nor do I have any desire to dig up the past. I don't feel the need to "get to the bottom" of anything. I knew enough to offer forgiveness, and that's all I needed to know.

My choice that morning as God laid out that Scripture before me was to dwell on all the good that God was doing—*or*—I could choose to think about that woman. It may seem like a small thing, even a natural response, and reasonable. The inquiries seemed justified. I could use a dismissive phrase like "I had a weak moment" or "I let my guard down." In reality, I had moved toward blatant rebellion. Whether I felt I deserved to know or not, God prompted me to do a certain thing and I didn't do it. That's sin. And I felt the effects of it immediately as I walked outside of God's protection.

Thank God for waking me the next morning with a new determination to keep going, as described in this verse I found: "Brothers and sisters, I do not consider myself yet to have taken hold of it. But one thing I do: Forgetting what is behind and straining toward what is ahead, I press on toward the goal to win the prize for which God has called me heavenward in Christ Jesus" (Phil. 3:13–14).

• Chapter 15 •

# Lavish Love

*I pray that you, being rooted and established in love,
may have power, together with all the Lord's holy
people, to grasp how wide and long and high and
deep is the love of Christ, and to know this love that
surpasses knowledge—that you may be filled to the
measure of all the fullness of God.*

EPHESIANS 3:17–19

The morning after my rainy meltdown, I felt prompted to write Micah a letter. Aunt Jan and Shannon must have slipped away early in the morning as they were already gone when I woke up. But when Aunt Jan stopped by to check on me that afternoon, I showed her the letter I had written. She shot me a raised eyebrow look. "I don't know how you can write this letter today," she said, shaking her head.

So I told her how I had awoken that morning with a new resolve to love my husband despite all that had happened. It was such a stark contrast to my feelings from the night before that I knew they were not my feelings at all. Mine had been full of despair, anger, jealousy, spite, and insecurity. When I woke up in the morning it was not about me anymore. I couldn't even think of myself because

I was so overwhelmed to share with Micah this fresh abundant love I had received for him.

I locked myself in the bathroom that morning and set to work writing the letter. I dare not bare to the world my intimate words that I shared with my husband that day. There is, however, one part that I feel compelled to share. I had written in the letter that morning, "I honestly don't think of you as a cheater. I think of you as my husband."

At the time I wrote this, of course, I had no idea I would ever be writing down our story in a book for all the world to see. It was for Micah. I could only imagine what he was thinking I thought about him. He had been awful, truly. But I had love for him, and I was desperate for him to understand that there was still hope for us.

He knew it didn't make sense for me to want him after everything I had been through. So I sincerely wanted him to know the truth. At that time, he was still "on the fence" about me. Early in the week, before my mental breakdown, I had asked him to make a decision about us and our marriage. I wanted to know if he was ready to make a commitment to me or if he still wanted a divorce. I realized I didn't want him to make that decision until he knew the facts. If he was going to leave me, he would do so fully knowing that he was giving up on someone who loved him. It was still his choice, but at least he would know.

I added at the end of the letter, "I know I can move forward with you." There was no room in my heart for doubt or bitterness because I was consumed with a passion to fight for him. If all I had to do was extend grace to Micah and then I got to be with him the rest of my life, I was eager to do so.

I felt like I was going to burst with anticipation. Since Micah works the night shift, he sleeps during the day, usually until around 3:00 p.m. I remember being anxious all day, waiting for him to wake up. I couldn't wait for him to receive the truth. I laid the letter on his pillow and asked him to read it whenever he felt ready.

When Micah did read the letter that day, he didn't respond at all. Finally, I asked him what he thought about it and he said simply, "It was nice." I was disappointed, sure. I felt the disappointment and I acknowledged it, but I didn't let it overtake me. I knew God had miraculously given me this blazing love I felt burning in my chest. I knew I couldn't have created or mustered up a love so intense. I had already become convinced that God was doing a great work behind the scenes, so it was hard to wallow in disappointment. See, when you become convinced God is doing something behind the scenes, it's hard to remain frantic.

So my big revelation didn't come from Micah that day. It came, once again, from God. During that season, as the battle for my marriage progressed, God began teaching me about his own love. He began to parallel the love I had for Micah with his love for me. He had given me this love, after all. It came from him, I knew it. He began to reveal to me that the overwhelming love and passion I had for Micah was just a taste of his own love for me, for all of us.

Let me stop right here and explain what I mean. I'm not saying I have learned to love like Christ all of the time, toward everyone. What I *am* saying, is that I believe God granted me a taste, a *portion*, of his relentless, perfect, overwhelming, selfless, pure, and sacrificing love for us. My love was geared toward my husband. But it was fierce and all-consuming, and it changed everything.

My whole life I believed the children's song "Jesus Loves Me." But it's hard to truly fathom or imagine a love unlike anything we have experienced before. Human love is so limited. It varies and shifts based on circumstances, based on feelings. And a lot of times, we love simply out of duty, obligation, or habit. We mean to do the right thing by someone but there is no fierceness behind it. No one is fighting for us. Having that season of fighting for Micah changed my whole perspective on God's love for us.

I fully understood that on my own, I wasn't capable of loving Micah with a perfect love. Not then. Not like that. There is no one on this earth who can convince me otherwise, that it was not Christ himself sharing his divine love with me for his purpose. He was showing me his love for me by letting me feel it, having it burn in my own heart toward someone else. I began to see, through that dim mirror, the depths of his love.

The following Wednesday I went back to Bible study with Shannon and her husband, John. On the ride home, I became utterly convinced I needed to tell Micah that I forgave him and exactly what I intended to do about that. It was the longest car ride ever. I eagerly greeted Micah when I walked in the door and sat him down on the couch.

I told him I forgave him. I explained how I understood that when God forgives me he doesn't throw anything back in my face again. He buries it and doesn't bring it back up. He doesn't ask questions about the extent of my sin or badger me with prolonged conversations about the details, nor does he care to explore the depths of it.

I told Micah I would not ask him any questions regarding what happened. I told him about how I had been controlling my mind and not only would I not talk about it, but that I was working very diligently not even to think about it. I was essentially banishing those thoughts from my mind. He was forgiven. It was in the past and covered in grace. It was no more.

I had known about forgiveness, of course, but now with a supernatural glimpse into God's level of forgiveness, I had a new level of understanding. I had pictured forgiveness as a wrong that was dismissed, but that the stain of the sin lingered over the person as a reminder. The sin was there, but overlooked. With this new concept of forgiveness I was experiencing, the sin wasn't overlooked. *It was gone.*

Micah sat with me that night as I talked to him about forgiveness and he was very quiet, as he was in those weeks. He didn't say much of anything. I had no idea what he was thinking in that moment, yet I went to bed that night feeling like a champion. I had never had that much capacity to love in my heart before, and it was truly exhilarating. I felt empowered enough to conquer the whole world.

It wasn't until the next day that I felt foolish. It hit my gut like a ton of bricks. Micah had never asked for my forgiveness! What if he didn't even want it? He never even said he would stop the thing he was doing! What if he was not sorry? What if he thought I was such a loser for presuming he wanted me and my forgiveness anyway? I felt so mortified at myself that I actually went back to Micah and "amended" my statement from the night before. In my fear of rejection, I told him that the forgiveness offer still stood *if he wanted it* and that I still meant every word.

In my hurry to gush love on Micah, I left out that tiny detail of waiting for him to come to me and want me. I thought Micah would be liberated by my offer. *Who gets that kind of a chance for a clean slate? Of course he would want that, right? He would want me, right?* But I did not know where I stood with him, and I felt extremely vulnerable for laying it all out there and being so eager to pardon anything and everything, only to be faced with the possibility of rejection.

It was soon after that happened that God started turning things around on me once again. He began paralleling my love for Micah with his love for me. Not for the first time, I realized that if God was indeed giving me a portion of his own love, that must reflect how he feels toward me, toward all of us. I was beginning to think this whole thing was one big giant object lesson to teach me about the depths and pureness of God's love.

Is he so eager to dump his grace on me that he can hardly wait for me to make it to him and ask for it? Yes. Is he giddy with anticipation for me to "get home" to share with me the good news that his love is unfaltering? Yes. Does he see my failure as an opportunity to demonstrate to me his dedication and loyalty and capacity to forgive? Yes. Is he hoping I will see that even when I fail him he is still unwilling to leave me? Yes. And this God who knows all things, from whom nothing is hidden, even what is done in secret, *when he looks at me*, does he see my sin? No. He only sees his daughter. Amazing.

I have heard people describe God's love before. But now, since this amazing love had flooded my own heart, this *lavish love* and this grace that is so *eager* to restore has been present in my own understanding, I became overcome with emotion. *My God, is that how you love me?* I took a few days processing this and marveling at the sheer dimensions and depths of it all.

And *why?* Why all this trouble? For nothing other than only wanting to be with me? I thought back to why I was fighting so hard for Micah. I wanted him back. I missed him. I simply wanted to be with him. I wanted to spend my whole life with him.

It wasn't about convenience, finances, our kids, what people might possibly think of me, or any other logical reason. There was no agenda. At this point it wasn't about what Micah was going to do for me. Rather, I simply wanted to be near him. He is a pleasure to me. He is a part of me. I would miss him and forever have a gap in my heart if he were absent from me. He was my husband, my friend, my person. And I truly believed that it would be better for him in the long run to accept this forgiveness and love from me than going down any other road.

Ya'll know at this point how I deal. Armed with this new heart revelation, I once again went to my knees before God. I knew that regardless of Micah's choice to love me or not to love me, to divorce me or not, I already stood secure in a love that was unbreakable, unavoidable, lavish, and complete. I understood just a part of the sincerity of God's great, amazing, consuming love.

First Corinthians 13:12 says, "For now we see in a mirror dimly, but then face to face. Now I know in part; then I shall know fully, even as I have been fully known" (ESV). As overwhelming as the new revelation of love for me was, I understood my love for Micah was only a small fraction of Christ's love for me, for every one of us. I only know and love in part. I only see dimly, whereas God is complete and perfect already. I knelt down and quieted myself before God, trying to wrap my head around the depths of his love.

I realized this revelation should not be so mind blowing. I should love my own husband, for goodness' sake. Why was this brand new information to me? Why was this concept explosive and rocking my world? I have known these truths in my head, but until those moments I did not truly begin to grasp the severity of what God has charged us to do when he said to love one another. It was life-changing in my marriage. But while Jesus was walking on this earth, he charged us with loving each other. Not just our spouses, but our family, community, those far away, panhandlers, politicians, addicts, celebrities, refugees. *Love each other.*

"A new command I give you: Love one another. As I have loved you, so you must love one another" (John 13:34). *Is this what he meant?* The thought took my breath away. Oh, how I have missed the mark! As disheartened as I was at never before understanding in my heart the severity and fierceness of Christ's love, I also felt absurdly excited to start showing this love to others. What if I applied these principles that I have learned to the rest of the world?

What if I used my 1 Corinthians 13 Love Filter on everyone I came into contact with? What if I showed patience to people who make a complete nuisance of themselves? What if I forgave that person who offended me instead of holding onto bitterness? What if I responded kindly to someone when they were downright wrong or rude? What if I disregarded my own vulnerability and lavished love on someone even at the risk of being rejected? What if I turned my attention to a complete stranger? What if I disregarded cultural and political lines and sincerely loved people simply because they are created by God?

In Matthew 22:37, Jesus says, "Love the Lord your God with

all your heart and with all your soul and with all of your mind." I believe that only when we cozy up next to the Father and love him first can we truly have the capacity to love others in this way. The ability to love like him comes from him. Imagine if we all started loving as Christ did.

We quite literally have the potential to change the whole world.

# Chapter 16

# *This Is War*

*Finally, be strong in the Lord and in his mighty
power. Put on the full armor of God, so that you can
take your stand against the devil's schemes. . . . Stand
firm then, with the belt of truth buckled around
your waist, with the breastplate of righteousness in
place, and with your feet fitted with the readiness
that comes from the gospel of peace. In addition to
all this, take up the shield of faith, with which you
can extinguish all the flaming arrows of the evil one.
Take the helmet of salvation and the sword of the
Spirit, which is the word of God.*

EPHESIANS 6:10–11, 14–17

And so began the battle to renew my mind. Yes, I had been
granted new mercies and a fresh resolve to love Micah, but I
still had to get back into the trenches to fight. Each day presented
its own opportunities to become disheartened. But now, I went to
battle knowing that Jesus was by my side, and I now knew better
than to step outside his protective shelter.

In addition to Philippians 4:7–8, I also clung to Romans 12:2,
"Do not conform to the pattern of this world, but be transformed

by the renewing of your mind" and 2 Corinthians 10:5, "We take captive every thought to make it obedient to Christ." Seeds of doubt and insecurity tried to creep back in, sure. Temptation would always be there in some form or another. At first, the temptation to dwell on the past tried to penetrate my mind every day. That's why Scripture instructs us to "garrison and mount guard over your hearts and mind" (Phil. 4:7, AMPC). This is war. Why would you need to set a guard if there is no attacker?

At first, when attacks and temptations to doubt came at me, they were like flaming arrows piercing my heart. But I took up the shield of faith and struck back with the sword of the Spirit. Each time I refused to dwell on a destructive thought and replaced it with praise or God's Word, the easier it became to defeat them. The attacks began to diminish or cease altogether for a while. The longer I let my thoughts linger, however, the stronger the attacks became and the harder it was to defend myself.

I'm not going to lie and say it wasn't a constant mind battle at first. And when I say at first, I mean weeks and months at a time of constant fighting and taking control of my mind from those unwanted thoughts. At the time, it seemed like the constant pounding would never end. I felt that I would have to live the rest of my life in battle mode over my mind. It was exhausting.

For example, Micah often saw this other woman while he worked. Not even intentionally, she just lived close by, and they worked the same hours, so she was out and about when my kids and I were home asleep. So every time Micah went to work, that presented a challenge for me. Do I sit at home and fret and worry about it until I develop an ulcer? Do I allow fear and anxiety to completely seize my heart? Do I dread the evening hours so much that it ruins my whole day? Or do I turn my attention to the Lord in that time, use it wisely by reading the Bible and building my faith by seeing what God says about me?

I also relearned to play the guitar, something I hadn't done much since college. I spent time in the middle of the night playing songs to God, until there was no fear, no worry, and I would be filled with an absurd confidence. Not that everything was going to turn out perfectly in my marriage. But in God's presence, there is a serious perspective shift. When God floods your heart, you know he's really all you need. If Micah should leave our family and proceed with the divorce, that was the worst case scenario. But the best case scenario was already happening in my living room. God was still God and he was flooding my heart.

As real as those feelings were in the moment, the attacks were still strong at every turn. I was fighting a battle for my joy, for my peace. I refused to believe that someone else's beauty diminished my own value, or that because someone rejected me I was unlovable. I was fighting against depression. I was fighting against all negative thoughts about myself, my husband, and my marriage. I knew those negative things were not the truth God was speaking into my life. Instead, I deliberately chose to believe God's words, not my own. Once again I was faced with a choice to put my money where my mouth was. I said I believed God. So was I going to live like it, or not?

I include this part of my story to say that if you are in that place of battle and you understand those feelings, take heart. It does get better. I don't believe that time heals all wounds, but I do believe that God does. He is the Master Healer. He doesn't do anything halfway. I believe when we act in obedience to him and we stay diligent, we become stronger.

In the trenches of my warfare it seemed like the battle would never end. And truth be told, I still have to guard my thoughts. We are called to be diligent and watchful always, but I am not fighting the same battle I was at that time. I remember when a few days would pass and I realized I hadn't thought about the affair at all, but sometimes I'd still hear a nagging thought that seemed to come out of nowhere and test my guard. But just like in a physical battle, there is a time of warfare and a time of victory. God will not leave you alone on the front lines, nor will he leave you there forever.

. . .

I feel like it is important for me to note that God was the source of my strength at this time. However, just like Moses who leaned on Aaron and Hur, I too found myself leaning on the people that God had put around me. I could confess to them when I was dwelling on something that would cause me discouragement. When I confessed, the attacks seemed to lose their strength. It was out in the open then, exposed, not hiding in secret. Once the enemy is exposed, he will likely turn and run. He knows he's about to be shot at, and there is power in numbers. My little circle would pray together and battle with me. It's so much better knowing that if war is unavoidable, at least you are not a lone soldier.

I think before all of this happened, I may have had a bit of a hero complex. I was never comfortable asking for help. Now I believe God never intended us to go it alone. He provided these precious women to me. I could tell them when I was too exhausted to go on in my own strength anymore. They helped me in the battle for peace of mind by holding me accountable and encouraging me to be diligent in doing what God had told me to do.

With each battle won, with every flaming arrow quenched, with each step in obedience, my faith was increasing. Instead of "flaming arrows," my negative thoughts became what I called "pesky little gnats," because I realized that on their own they had no real power, they could only "buzz" and annoy and distract me. But I also knew it was only because of God that they seemed so insignificant. I had seen firsthand the power of the gnats when you let them in and then your thoughts take over and prevail. It is no good place, trust me. Gnats sent from the enemy's camp are meant to destroy and defeat you.

I have since heard story after story of people who have been through similar situations. Some of the women I have talked to really related to me when I talked about guarding my mind when I was attacked by "gnats." Either they related because they were able to find stillness and peace in God, or they hadn't found peace and they instead had to go through the aftereffects, much like my walk in the rain.

I have a friend named Lena whose husband had an affair and immediately was sorry for what he had done and had tried to repair their marriage. She confessed to me that she just couldn't get the affair out of her mind. She couldn't stop talking about it or asking questions. She wanted to talk about it until she was blue in the face. Their marriage ended in divorce.

A few years ago she married Justin, a friend of mine who also came out of a bitter divorce. His ex-wife had also had an affair and left him. Though Justin wasn't ready to give up on the marriage, she still went through with the divorce. So when Lena and Justin got married a few years later, they both had kids from their previous marriages.

I have watched their relationship bloom and have seen how their families have blended over the past few years. I know they love each other, and they are truly a beautiful couple with a beautiful blended family. But she sent me a text one day with such honesty that it caught me off guard.

It said: "You keep fighting! Fight for your family. Don't give up as easily as I did with mine. Not that I would trade Justin for anything, because I know he and I were meant for each other, but I couldn't let go of the hate and anger I felt toward [her ex-husband], and my kids are the ones that suffered with me being selfish and not forgiving him until after our divorce. I'm praying so hard for you. Blended family is not easy and [Justin's ex-wife] isn't happy. I so badly want to believe that Justin is happy. But it's still not ideal and certainly not the way any of us wants our lives to be."

The bluntness of her words shocked me. Those flaming arrows from the devil had hit their mark. They destroyed her peace of mind, and contributed to the break up of a marriage that ultimately separated a family. And although Lena had rebuilt her life, she realized now where she had stumbled. Even now, she regretted not controlling her mind.

The buzzing that seeks to destroy can sound like doubt, insecurity, hate, jealousy, and bitterness. You must take up your shield against those flaming arrows. You must refuse to allow those pesky gnats to take up time or space in your brain. If you listen to them, they will magnify until they take over and destroy any peace or sound mind that you could have.

These negative thoughts, these pesky flying gnats that buzz around my head looking for a way in, are as much of a temptation to me as any impure thoughts I imagined Micah could have been indulging in at the time. If I dwelled on the actions that had happened, I would not want to forgive or love Micah. God told me to do both.

Micah's unfaithfulness happened only for a short while, starting and ending within just a few weeks. Yet I could've played and replayed those images over and over in my mind, dozens, hundreds, or thousands of times. And for me, it would have happened over and over that many times. Just as traumatic, just as paralyzing, every time. It would have destroyed our relationship, without question. It could destroy us even today. I wouldn't have been able to offer forgiveness for something that was still going on (even if just in my mind).

My friend Kim sent me an excerpt from the devotional *Jesus Calling* that explains what I'm saying this way: "Rehearsing your troubles results in experiencing them many times, whereas you were meant to go through them when they actually occur. Do not multiply your suffering in this way!"[1]

I had a friend who became convinced her husband was cheating on her. He was partners with a woman at work and they were also friends. My friend's husband insisted there was nothing romantic going on at all, but my friend did not believe him. That led to panic. She started to doubt every little thing he did and became very suspicious and paranoid.

By the time she confided in me about it, she had decided it really was all in her mind, but it was a horrible thing to go through. It was traumatizing for her and because of it, she related to everything that happened to me when we talked about it. Because of the restlessness of her mind she experienced the same tormenting emotions I did, even though the adultery was only imaginary. It was horrible for her and it was all so unnecessary. That's just an example of the power of our minds. Beware of your thoughts. Guard against them. Place a lock guard around them. Be diligent. Do this every day.

I decided early on that Micah's decisions or failures could not affect the stability of my mental stillness. I knew I did not have the mental capacity to worry about where he was, what he could be doing, and thoughts he might be thinking. I only had the capacity and responsibility to guard my own mind (especially at the beginning, that alone was a full-time job!) I would be held accountable only for myself.

If I let fear or insecurity run rampant in my brain, it would destroy me, and God told me to keep myself whole and not to entertain those thoughts. So when I indulged in them, it became sin for me.

A few months later, after God had started the work toward restoring our marriage, we were doing a Bible study with Shannon and John at their house, and I shared how God had instructed me to take negative thoughts captive. John interrupted, "Stop right there." John looked at Micah and said, "As a police officer, when you arrest someone you are effectively taking them as your captive. Would you release a captive? What would happen if you released your captive?"

Micah responded, "They could turn against me. Depending on how dangerous he is, he could come after me. Ultimately he could kill me. I arrest him, secure him with handcuffs, and restrain him in the cruiser behind bars. Then I take him to jail to be detained."

John nodded as he made his point. "He is bound up, not free to run around loose as he pleases."

The Bible instructs us to take our thoughts captive. We act as though we have no control over our thoughts. We act as if once they pop into our heads, we have to let them live there. How deadly can they be anyway? They are invisible. They are just *thoughts. Everyone* has thoughts.

*Take them captive.* They will kill you.

This process of renewing my mind and swatting at the gnats, I emphasize again: *I had to do it every day.* No matter how much time has passed, when the thoughts attack me like an intruder, I pray they find me with my guard up, calling on Jesus. May they find me with songs in my head and Scriptures in my heart, fully guarded with the armor God has given me.

# Chapter 17

# *Up and Running*

> *Brothers and sisters, I do not consider myself yet to*
> *have taken hold of it. But one thing I do: Forgetting*
> *what is behind and straining toward what is ahead,*
> *I press on toward the goal to win the prize for which*
> *God has called me heavenward in Christ Jesus.*
> PHILIPPIANS 3:13–14

Days and weeks went by with no discernible change in our situation. Yes, Micah still lived with us. Yes, I continued to live out my 1 Corinthians 13 Love Filter and continued to battle negative thoughts. But a dismal Halloween came and went, and the holidays were fast approaching. Micah remained mostly closed off to me. Aloof. Distant.

I wanted to fix everything instantly. This waiting around was really for the birds. I wanted answers, to know what my future would look like. I wanted a solution, resolution for my marriage. But it was all outside of my control. God had called me to wait. To be patient.

Ugh.

Conditioned by our fast-food, pill-popping culture, all too often we want a "quick fix" for whatever issue we are facing. We are in a hurry. We have little self-discipline. Because of our impatience, oftentimes we miss out on God's best for us. We get tired of waiting and give up, mid-journey. We want our gratification if not instantly, then as soon as possible. We fail to realize during the tough times that God wants to teach us something. Not just *some*thing, but *multiple* things! Who he is. Who we are. What he's done for us. What we need to change. Those weeks for me were a crash course in character building, a post-doctorate in self-discipline. And sometimes, I must admit, my Divine Tutor seemed a harsh taskmaster, loading on the homework and demanding the impossible.

One thing I learned is that when God asks us to exercise discipline in any area of our lives, *there will be pain!* Always. Discipline takes endurance. It demands consistency. It takes practice and patience, and it hurts! I recently ran across this quote by C. S. Lewis: "I didn't go to religion to make me happy. I always knew a bottle of port would do that. If you want a religion to make you feel really comfortable, I certainly don't recommend Christianity."[1]

• • •

When I started running, I was learning to enjoy discipline. In those forty-five minutes of my day I could blast my music and duke it out with God. He had asked me to do something that felt ginormous to me, to give him my broken and mangled heart and entrust to him a future that seemed bleak and hopeless. Outwardly it seemed impossible.

Over the years, I had often been told I looked like a runner, that I had an athlete's body. But I didn't play sports in school and was not coordinated, nor athletic. Running was not something I had ever done, and keeping up with three boys felt like enough of a workout. At the end of a busy day I just wanted to reward myself with a warm brownie and cold milk, thanks.

But I felt like God was pushing me to my limits in this other area of my life, where he was asking me to guard my heart, to have faith, to take authority over my thoughts and words, and to trust him in a situation where doing so seemed impossible. I felt extremely vulnerable. I had also never realized (in practice) that love (the verb) required discipline. I'm not talking about attraction, the mushy kind of love that we *feel*, but the love that is described in 1 Corinthians 13. It is quite the challenge! It is not natural. It takes *discipline*.

I knew this challenge was stretching me beyond what I thought I was capable of, and running seemed equally as daunting and impossible. I had never done it before. It hurt to run. It hurt after the run. It hurt the next day. It hurt the day after that. Plus, it was just *hard*. It was exhausting.

As I would push myself to go farther, to go longer, to not stop until I met my goal, I felt as though my lungs would explode. *My body was against me!* If you have ever trained for a race or even started out running like I did, you probably know what that feels like. Especially when you are a beginner and out of shape. You feel like you can't breathe. You think you can't go on. Your body begs to stop. It screams to rest. Plus, *did I say this already?* You really feel like you can't breathe! Something in your brain registers this as important. It presents quite the conflict between your brain and your legs.

I don't even remember initially why I started running. But I began to enjoy conquering something. I began to enjoy feeling like I was going to die . . . and then evading death! My body screamed at me that I was going to die if I kept going. *There was joy in discovering it was lying!*

Something happened in my soul when I realized that what was going on in my physical body was paralleling the hidden, inside work that God was doing in me. He was showing me that the principle of discipline is the same in the physical world as it is the spiritual one. When we exercise discipline in our lives, change is inevitable.

He was giving me the encouragement I needed to know that my emotions, my feelings, and even my physical body *do not control me*. We as humans have the ability to exercise discipline. And even then, when we fall short, as heirs with Christ, we can tap into his supernatural strength. And he helps us.

> *Israel, why then do you complain*
> > *that the LORD doesn't know your troubles*
> > *or care if you suffer injustice?*
> *Don't you know? Haven't you heard?*
> *The LORD is the everlasting God;*
> > *he created all the world.*
> *He never grows tired or weary.*
> > *No one understands his thoughts.*
> *He strengthens those who are weak and tired.*
> *Even those who are young grow weak;*
> > *young people can fall exhausted.*
> *But those who trust in the LORD for help*
> > *will find their strength renewed.*
> *They will rise on wings like eagles;*
> > *they will run and not get weary;*
> > *they will walk and not grow weak.*
>
> ISAIAH 40:27–31 GNT

As I trained my body, I also began to eat healthier. I couldn't eat whatever I wanted and then have the strength and endurance to run every day. I began to crave things that were good for me and would fuel my new-found passion. When I cut back on sugar and ate raw fruits and veggies instead of my usual processed meals, I felt more energetic and ready to run. One evening I was taking a shower and I looked down at my body and screamed, "My love handles are gone!"

As I persistently conditioned my body, it began to submit to the discipline. Seeing the transformation of my physical body was so encouraging. It was as if God was assuring me, saying, "Things are happening, you are changing. You can't see into the spiritual realm to see all the things that I am doing, but you can see this. Just as your physical body is changing, so is your spiritual reality. Transformation is happening. I am working. Don't give up."

The principle of discipline works in both the physical and spiritual realms. Exercising discipline in the spiritual realm produces change just as much as exercising discipline in the natural world produces change. In the physical world, if you significantly reduce the amount of sugar and calories you eat, consistently make healthy food choices, and exercise daily, you will reap physical benefits. Change is inevitable.

The same goes for spiritual discipline. It's a bit more challenging for us, though, because we can't always see or test the progress like we can in the natural world. But *discipline equals change*. Discipline in the spiritual world can look like obeying God consistently, even when we don't feel like it. Even when the results don't look like the results we thought we should have gotten. Yet blessings will follow obedience, and obedience takes discipline. When God tells us to do something and we obey him, the harvest of that is assured.

Shannon kept speaking this phrase to me over and over during this season: "Obedience puts you in a posture to receive your blessing." There is a reason God has told us to take our thoughts captive and to control our tongues. These are forms of spiritual discipline. When we consistently follow his guidelines, victory is certain.

Paul explains the need for self-discipline: "Do you not know that in a race all the runners run, but only one gets the prize? Run in such a way as to get the prize. Everyone who competes in the games goes into strict training. They do it to get a crown that will not last, but we do it to get a crown that will last forever. Therefore I do not run like someone running aimlessly; I do not fight like a boxer beating the air. No, I strike a blow to my body and make it my slave so that after I have preached to others, I myself will not be disqualified for the prize" (1 Cor. 9:24–27).

For me, running was a physical token God gave me to hold onto. It was a promise. "You trust me with this, and in the physical you can see the changes. Continue to trust in me, and the spiritual world will also align to my will."

Around that time, Switchfoot released their song "Love Alone Is Worth the Fight." Jon Foreman, the lead singer, did a *Behind the Music* interview on the radio, and when asked about the song, he said, "You can't be a lover without being a fighter."

That is what I took to the streets. I ran mostly outside (you know, *in public*) and things would get a little intense. God had instructed me to be kind, to be patient, yet I was in a battle. I was fighting for my husband. At home I needed to be calm and show quiet strength. But outside during my run, the fight was on!

At some point, delirium would set in. Running for me was an outward expression of endurance, of the inner challenge I was going through. When my body would scream at me to stop, I would scream back, "No!" It was no longer about running. At that point, it was about remaining obedient to God. It was about my husband. It was about my family. Each mile I ran proclaimed, "I will not give up! I won't quit on this man, I will continue to love, to pray, to endure! I will be faithful to the task God has entrusted to me. I don't care that it hurts!"

I would blare music through my earbuds and sometimes I would cry as I ran. Sometimes as I ran I would gain a surge of hope and I would laugh out loud or high-five branches that were within reach of the running path, as if they were placed there by God to cheer me on. Sometimes my spirits would be so lifted by a song's lyrics I would loudly shout in agreement or raise my fist in some secret victory.

I wondered what people must have thought of this crying,

shouting lunatic. To make it worse, I have a winking problem. Sometimes I wink at random strangers and make it nice and awkward for them. I don't mean to do this. It kind of just occurs, like smiling at a stranger. I sometimes caught myself doing this to people when I ran by them.

I winked at a confused stranger as I passed by as if just to let them know, "Hey. I've got a secret. God has asked me to do the impossible. But don't worry. It's gonna be okay. He's with me. Hopefully this encourages you in your own battle. Go get 'em! We got this!"

See, I can't say all that to a stranger in the middle of a long run. So I wink at him and nod my head as if we have gained an understanding. I most certainly come across as a complete crazy.

*Whatever.* Let them look. Let them gawk. Let them think whatever they want. They don't know the task before me, nor the battle I'm fighting! They don't know that this is not about the running. They don't know that everything I love is at stake. They probably don't know that God is with me, providing me with strength. So they probably don't know I will soon be a champion.

• Chapter 18 •

# Basking

*Let us then with confidence draw near to the throne
of grace, that we may receive mercy and find grace to
help in time of need.*

HEBREWS 4:16 ESV

In November, Micah had agreed to regularly attend marriage counseling with Shannon and John. They had recently been asked by the lead pastor of their church to head up a ministry for young couples, which I found convenient. I believe we were technically their "first case." It wasn't until I reached out to Shannon that she told me they had recently been trained and commissioned by their pastor for this new position. Guess God didn't want to break them in easy to their new ministry since he handed them our train wreck as a welcome package!

John and Shannon were convinced that although our marriage was in shambles, if we chased after God as individuals, our marriage would fall into proper place by default. Before Micah and I began chasing God together as a couple, I had to chase him for myself.

I've talked so much about God's presence sustaining me at that time, describing it as being kept in a "bubble." I played praise and worship music all day long. Yes, it's uplifting and it's faith-building. But also, it was my secret move, a strategic plan to chase after God. You see, sometimes as the music played and I worshipped, there would be a shift in dimensions. I would be in my kitchen, or living room, or bathroom, or car, and the tiny hairs on my arms would start to prick up. I would sense a familiar wind. But it's not a wind you can feel or that blows your hair. It's a presence that causes me to pause, to stop dead in my tracks. *Is it you?* I dare not move. A knowing smile finds my lips. *Yes.* And I prepare to be swept away.

For me, playing praise and worship music is like loitering outside of the CEO's office door all day long. Eventually that door might open and I might get to slip inside. I might be brought in and be allowed to have conversation with the man in charge. I could be brought into "the know" of the corporation, weaseling my way in to hang with the big dogs.

Sometimes when I worship, I simply feel my spirit lifted and rejuvenated as I lift up my King. Other times though, and I can't say when or why or how—since it's of his choosing—I am completely swept away.

I've often heard it said that in worshipful moments like these, we are *basking* in God's glory. That is such churchy terminology to me. It seems to me that wording like that would be an automatic turnoff when talking to anyone other than your Sunday school teacher.

Who would understand that term unless they themselves have basked? It's hard for humans to describe being in the presence of God. It's an invisible place. There you are, sometimes so overcome that you are brought to your knees in humility before a holy God, bowed down. Most of the time for me, I am overcome with reverence. Quiet and still, awestruck, a holy fear of being so near my Creator.

Other times you could catch me smiling, laughing, dancing like David did in the streets (probably looking quite like a lunatic), or crying. I'm good for the crying. It can be a very embarrassing place if you are "caught" or someone walks in on you unaware while you are basking.

That's because we are spiritual beings in a physical world. You can't see the basking. It's very hard to explain. And explaining it using human words always seems to lessen the experience. How do you explain being in the presence of the Almighty? If you've been there yourself, you already know. If you have not, please pardon my feeble attempt. There is just so much lacking in human words.

It is nothing like this, but since there is nothing to compare it to, just imagine with me. You close your eyes and you are gliding amidst a colorful sunset. The wind is warm and cozy, yet crisp, and beckons for adventure. Desire is awakened and something sparks the sleeping soul alive. You see beauty. You are breathing in mystery and are breathless with expectation. But it is not a place or a thing where you are headed.

You feel the strength of his almighty arm. You are compelled to believe anything is possible in his grasp. You glance around solar systems flecked with new colors you've never seen before. The whole wonder of the universe, the majesty of everything that is beautiful in creation you have sprawled before your eyes. You are overcome with wonder and awe, speechless. Excitement stirs your racing heart. You are eager for something.

Then, there is a shift. From your tour of the universe you are plopped into the dark, into the quiet, but not alone. A tangible presence. You can't see anything else. You don't care. It's intimate now. This God of the entire universe and vast expanses of worlds never even explored has closed the door to all of that. You're glad that's all faded now because this is better. You are full. You realize all of the searching in your whole life has been for this moment. The created meets with the Creator.

You dare not breathe. You don't want to open your eyes, to bump anything, to make this go away. *Don't go away.* It's the intimacy of a lover, a friend, a father, but none of those, because this love is perfect.

That would be my first attempt to describe my secret meetings. Instead we just say, "We bask in his presence." Bask is an odd word. And it's not enough. I looked it up to try and see just what my problem is with this word.

> **"Bask"** (verb - usually followed by *in*)
> to lie in or be exposed to pleasant warmth, especially
> that of the sun
> to flourish or feel secure under some benevolent influ-
> ence or favorable condition

I love the initial dictionary explanation of the word *bask*: "to lie in or be exposed to pleasant warmth."[1] *To lie* there. Not a hurried, frenzied moment simply visiting to demand something or to gain an answer from God, but a time to simply lie in his presence. Just lie there. Be near him. Be exposed to him. Do you even know what that exposure has the ability to accomplish? I may not fully know the impact these moments of quiet lying with him have truly done for me, but I can feel it burning in my soul.

There is no condition more favorable than knowing the security you learn while lying there, being exposed to God's presence. You become changed in those moments, whether you realize it or not. Without effort, you begin to flourish under his breath. **Flourish.** "To be in a vigorous state; to grow luxuriantly."[2] **Luxuriant.** "Abundant or lush in growth; richly abundant; lacking restraint."[3] Think about what being exposed to the presence of this Creator does to a human soul.

It jolts the sleeping spirit alive and frequent visits sustain this quest for wholeness. I know that God's presence healed me. It is the very same presence that convinced Peter, who left his career to follow this man Jesus after just one encounter. It is the same persuasive presence that urges me to drop all my demands of the day and simply follow him wherever he is. Wherever he is headed, I want to go too.

In these moments I feel convinced to abandon whatever cockamamie plans I have for myself and give whatever I have, however meager, to pursue whatever tasks he gives me. Just like Peter, the pursuits I had before I met this Jesus seem unfulfilling and dull now.

I have since changed my mind about this word *bask*. It still sounds like an odd thing to say, "to bask" in God's presence or his glory. Yet it seems pretty accurate if you have to pick just one word. Without basking in the presence of God, I don't know where I would be. What would have become of me?

John spoke to me very sternly at the very beginning of this journey. They had come over to my house and found me sitting on my couch sniffling and crying and still in shock. John said, "What you are going through can cause you to break. Look at me!" He glared into my eyes. "The enemy would want nothing more than to turn you into a sniveling, desperate, broken little girl. There's nothing attractive about that. Do not let that happen. You are a daughter of the King. Listen to what God says about you, not what the enemy would have you to believe. Listen to God. Lean on him."

How could I hear what God was saying about me? How could I get away from the actual words I was hearing out loud, coming from my circumstance? By shutting out the world. By going before God himself and quieting my soul before him. By basking.

In those dark days I heard my husband say, "I am not attracted to you." "I don't love you." "There is a better option out there for me than you." He was essentially trying to throw me out with the trash. God said, "Ummm, no." I don't want to quote God directly on that, but he said something like that. And he began to show me evidence of his glory.

The Bible study we did together was called *Chase* by Jennie Allen. In it, she describes God's glory as "evidence of God on earth." [4] By spending time there, in his glory, I became changed. When you see evidence of something, it solidifies your belief. It proves it. Just like in court. If you want a group of jurors to believe something one way or the other, you present them the evidence. *That must be true because there is the evidence.*

In my quest for more of God, in these moments of basking, my faith was actually being built because I was sitting in the evidence room. I saw it. I knew it to be true. I walked away with my faith stronger, solidified. There is not a person in this world that could convince me that my invisible meetings did not happen, that this God I rely on is not real. He met with me. He changed me. He solidified my belief.

During that Bible study, we also looked at the story of David and Goliath from 1 Samuel 17. I have always admired David in that story. The audacity, boldness, and confidence a young shepherd boy had in his Creator is really something worth examining. To march up to the giant Goliath unintimidated. To charge toward this massive warrior with abandon, risking his life so fearlessly. It's a thrilling tale.

David didn't even have the stones for his slingshot at the time he became enraged at Goliath for taunting his God. He had already started down the path to fight Goliath and was gaining momentum when he grabbed some rocks from the creek bed, almost as an afterthought. *I have God on my side,* he must have thought. He had to know that to be so empowered. *Oh yeah, and I need to stop and get stones for my slingshot.* He knew the main thing he needed was God. His confidence was not in the weapons he had.

David was amazing. The true champion, the hero of the story. He was favored by God and hailed by all the people for such an amazing victory.

Unfortunately, as I heard this story told again, I related to his brothers and with the cowering crowd of onlooking soldiers. *How ridiculous they must have looked to David.* David knew that the mighty God of the universe, who spins the planets, was on their side. He had true faith in his God. *What in the world are they afraid of?* he must have thought. I imagine him shrugging his shoulders at their fear and then going out and, almost without effort, slaying the giant that had the armies trembling.

How ridiculous I must look most of the time. Professing to serve this same mighty God of David, and yet living most of my life in fear, too intimidated to go for greatness. When God did move on my behalf, I was so shocked and amazed that I felt like waving my arms and shouting from the rooftop, "Look what God did for me! It's a miracle!"

I imagine David would chide, "Well, of course he did a miracle. You serve a God of miracles! You are finally beginning to understand God, lesson 101. Welcome to your faith."

# Chapter 19

# Micah

*Do not gloat over me, my enemy!*
*Though I have fallen, I will rise.*
*Though I sit in darkness,*
*the LORD will be my light.*

MICAH 7:8

Micah grew up in the home of a drug addict. His mother became addicted to pain killers while she was in her twenties, so he doesn't remember her being any other way. When he was still a child, she moved on to more extreme drugs. His childhood consisted of his mother chasing one high after another. She moved the kids around from state to state and from school to school. When they finally settled in Chillicothe, the only constant thing in the home was the inconsistency. Random people popped in and out of the house, sometimes crashing on couches, the beds, and floors.

Though Micah had other half siblings he periodically visited, his home consisted of his mother and younger sister. It was not uncommon for the children to be left alone for days at a time. He recalls one particular time at around five years old, three days had passed and his mother still had not returned home. He had been left alone with his three-year-old sister. The fridge and cupboards remained mostly empty, and he remembers wondering why they never had food in the house, since he knew they received tickets that were like cash for free food. Yet he was hungry.

Many of the stories I know about my husband's childhood I learned many years after we were married. These stories I learned from his father's side of the family, who had tried to gain custody of the children while they were young, but to no avail.

One of the saddest stories they told me was that one night a pickup truck pulled up into the driveway of the farmhouse. His grandma and aunts were in the kitchen when they saw the headlights coming up the lane. A man they did not know was driving the truck. In the back bed of the pickup were Micah and his sister. They were very young at the time, not even school age. The driver explained that their mother was at a party nearby and had passed out or became too incoherent to care for the children. Someone at the party knew the kids had family down the road so they told him to take the kids there.

Once during elementary school, Micah came home from school to find that his mother had overdosed. When Micah entered the house after school that day, it looked like a crime scene. Beside his mother was an empty bottle of pills and a note. The note had already been discovered by his little sister, who had arrived home from school first. His little sister saw the note and pills and assumed their mom was dead. Wanting to be with her mother, she took the rest of the bottle.

Micah picked up his little sister, who was laying lifeless, and carried her to a neighbor's house who immediately sent for an ambulance. Both mother and daughter had their stomachs pumped at the hospital that day. Even after that event, the children remained in the home.

●  ●  ●

I cannot even imagine my kids being exposed to the horrors those kids had to endure even for one day. Micah rarely talked about any of it. When we did talk about it, he wasn't angry, he wasn't sad. He felt no hard feelings. He was just numb. That's why when the numbness spilled over into our marriage, I just assumed there was no changing it. He had learned at an early age to cope by not feeling.

In the days leading up to the affair, while I was attending the conference in Columbus, an opportunity to feel presented itself to Micah. A woman whom Micah found himself attracted to appeared back into his life. For the first time in a long time, he began feeling again. He felt attraction. He felt excitement. He also felt nervous, but even that was a feeling!

He recalls going for a run one night while I was away, and being very honest with God. He was angry, fed up with being numb, and intrigued by these feelings. He wanted to feel. He was tired of feeling nothing. Angrily, he said to God, "If you don't stop me, I'm doing this. I'm going to enter into this relationship." He was defiant and rebellious, and he felt.

He chased the feeling. He decided feeling anything would be worth the backlash. *People get divorced all the time*, he reasoned. *Shauna will get over it. The kids will be fine.*

The next day after Micah's talk with the Lord, Shannon's husband John showed up on our front doorstep. (We were not close with John and Shannon at this time so no one could have known what was running through Micah's mind.) This visit was a divine intervention.

Micah answered the door and John stood there looking stern. "You ok, brother?" John asked suspiciously. Then he continued, "I don't know why, but I cannot get you out of my mind these last few days. The Lord told me to come over here and check on you." Micah shrugged him off, thanked him for the visit, and went on with his day. Looking back, however, we see God weaving his ever-present hand of grace all throughout our story.

After Micah sat me down and had "the talk" in which he asked me for a divorce, in his mind that's just what would happen. Our relationship was done. The relationship with the other woman began. He thought he knew what to expect—an irrational, crazed, and angry soon-to-be ex-wife. His phone would be flooded with outraged texts from "her side" friends and family. His family would certainly, at least initially, reject him and the decision he was making to divorce his wife.

Contrary to all the backlash he was so certain would happen, none of it did. Instead, he was faced with the most difficult thing to accept when you know you are unworthy: he was forced to stare at grace head on.

During that same time, God had me cornered in my secret place. I was overwhelmed with love for Micah and used him as my guinea pig for following this new Love Filter I had found: "Love is patient, love is kind. It does not envy, it does not boast, it is not proud. It does not dishonor others, it is not self-seeking, it is not easily angered, it keeps no records of wrongs." Empowered by the Holy Spirit as I strived to reflect these words, I was able to put aside my normal nature and take on one that resembled more of Christ's.

Beyond Micah's surprise at my reaction, he was also taken aback by the silence. No one was blowing up his phone and condemning him. Word of the affair did not spread around like wildfire. The few people who came forward only did so in love, in the same spirit of grace that was leading all of us who were close to him in that season.

In early November, Aunt Jan came over with her tiny, black, leather-bound Bible. Her Bible has more Scripture verses highlighted than not, with notes scribbled around each page of text and the leather is worn from hours of study. She sat at our kitchen table with Micah and prophesied. I did not sit in on this meeting; he told me about it after the fact.

God had led her to verses to share with him, and a clear warning she was to give. She told me later she wrestled with giving away such a strong word. But she couldn't shake God's heavy leading, so she obediently arrived at our home in submission to God.

She told him the decisions he was making were a matter of life and death. She didn't know if it was spiritual death or actual death, but she was convinced Satan was out to destroy him. Trust me when I say a word from Aunt Jan will not be shrugged off easily. She read from Habakkuk and spoke with the authority of an Old Testament prophet. Her talk was stern, but came from a place of immense love and concern she had for him. God was setting the stage of redemption for this man.

It was a few days after Aunt Jan's talk that I began noticing cracks in Micah's hardened heart. I began to recognize moments of softness toward me. These moments did not always last, and I didn't know if I could expect them to come back, so when he showed a softness to me, and a willingness to talk, I tried to make good use of those moments.

That evening, after the kids were in bed, I found him sitting in our kitchen nook, listening to music. I pulled up a stool and sat beside him. When I spoke to him, he responded gently, so I knew I had caught him in a good moment. The lights were dim and our house was quiet. "Our anniversary is coming up," I began. Then I made a proposal, "Do not make any decision about the fate of our marriage until then. End all communication with the other woman for now, at least, and give us a chance to work on us. We could go back to California for our anniversary trip. We could leave the kids with my grandparents, pull money from our savings account." I rambled all of these things. We would never have taken a trip like this before. We wouldn't have justified spending that kind of money for one week. "I know it'll be a lot of money, but you'll lose half of everything if you divorce me anyway," I added for good measure.

To my absolute disbelief and delight, he agreed to all of it. He got online and even booked our flight that very night while I sat beside him, so I didn't have to worry about him changing his mind the next day. It was paid for, we were going. He booked the trip for the week of November 16–23. That also happened to be the week of my birthday. I felt at peace, knowing that no matter what happened in the days between now and then, at least we would have that week together. I was filled with new relief and hope and wondered what God was going to do now. I knew God was up to something. I could see bits and pieces of something starting to take shape, but I couldn't see the big picture.

• • •

Shannon told me about a conversation she had with Micah one day when he had gone to her house for a haircut. She had him seated on a stool in the middle of her kitchen with a cape draped around his shoulders. They were talking about his mother. Micah and Shannon have the same dad, but different mothers. Shannon, being older, has her own memories of Micah's mom. Shannon said, "Do you remember what your mom used to be like?" He answered her matter of factly. "No. I don't. I just remember an incredibly selfish person. She missed everything. She wasn't there when we were kids and she's not around now for her grandkids."

Shannon continued with her own memories. "Yes, but I am talking about before that. *She had a life*, she had so much potential. She was beautiful and fun, and would light up the room when she walked into it." Unfortunately, Micah never got to see that side.

My own memory of her is mostly the same as Micah's: half-coherent, slurred speech, falling asleep every few minutes, a recluse. I can still see her sitting in her recliner in a poorly lit room, alone. She burned nearly every bridge she crossed, hurting so many people along the way to filling her ever-pressing need to numb herself. It was a very sad existence, and sad memories, indeed.

"What was her problem, Micah?" Shannon whispered. "Her

problem?" Micah repeated, "She was a drug addict, that was her problem," he responded shaking his head at the simple question. Shannon continued, "No, I mean the initial problem, before that. Her problem was that the enemy tricked her into thinking she had nothing to lose, and she lost everything."

Micah's mom died before this book was completed. I wasn't going to add these stories about her while she was living, because we always believed there could be a chance for her to experience forgiveness and the exhilarating thrill of being reborn by the power of Jesus while she lived on this earth.

But while she lived, she claimed she was fine. Second Timothy 3:5 says in the last days people will be having "a form of godliness but denying its power." She claimed she was a follower of Jesus. Yet she lived a very shallow life, one with no real power. If we ever recommended she receive treatment, she would act completely confused. "Why?" she would respond. "I don't have a problem." You can't fix a problem you don't admit you have. She was a bluffer.

We had that in common.

• Chapter 20 •

# Bluffer

*But he said to me, "My grace is sufficient for you, for
my power is made perfect in weakness." Therefore I
will boast all the more gladly about my weaknesses,
so that Christ's power may rest on me.*

2 CORINTHIANS 12:9

I kept noticing odd things happening all around me. I began to
take note of those things after Aunt Jan began coming over to
check in on me regularly after I hit rock bottom that one rainy
night. She said to me one day, "You keep saying that was *odd*, and
this was *odd*. Watch out for those things, that you don't overlook
them, especially at this time when God is speaking so clearly to
you. It makes me wonder how often he tries to use these odd things
to get our attention and how many times we overlook him."

I believe I was only noticing those things because I felt hyper-
sensitive to the Holy Spirit. And at that point I remembered an
odd thing that had happened the weekend of the conference.
Remember, the conference took place only days before Micah asked
me for a divorce.

During that weekend, I attended a workshop about creativity
in kid's ministry. The speaker, Patty Smith, told us a story about

her daily routine. She said she started her day with a workout. At this point she knelt down on the floor and stuck a line of blue tape on the floor. Next, she had her morning coffee and answered emails (more tape behind her). Then she made breakfast and drove the kids to school (tape on the floor to her side), worked in her office and attended meetings (more tape), picked her kids up and prepared dinner (more tape down), checked and answered more emails (tape), and then she got ready for bed and started it all over again in the morning (tape). By the end of her story she had created the shape of a "box" with the tape on the floor and she was standing inside of it.

She said, "See what has happened? I have boxed myself in. Yet my *job* is to help people to be *more* creative! And here I struggle with being boxed in every day." She instructed us to get into groups and talk about what we liked or didn't like about our "box" (daily routines) and to brainstorm creative ways we could break out of it.

Guess what? I was the only person at our table who smiled and said, "I like my box." I even felt a bit sorry for the other team members who wished they could break out of their own boxes and be more free and adventurous. *Those poor dears. I'm so glad I have it all together over here.*

While Micah went through the police academy and before he was employed with our city's police department, I worked at our local hospital. Although I liked my job, my heart longed to be at home with our kids. Gabe was just a baby at the time and I felt like I was missing so much of our kids' lives by being away from home during the day. After a few years of working full time, I got to stay home with them, so I was thankful for all the mundane little tasks that came with being a stay-at-home mom. I enjoyed my routine with the kids. I liked my box.

Well, as you know, the very next day after "the box" discussion, my neat and tidy little box collapsed!

Talk about a wake-up call.

Now I feel the need to clarify: I'm not saying it's a bad thing to be thankful for what you have! Thankfulness is necessary! But you've probably heard the saying, "More of the same, gets you more of the same." If I am fully satisfied with everything in my immediate sphere and have no goals to change anything, I never will. I already explained how complacent in my spiritual walk I had become. I was living only minimally for God, and I was fine with it.

I don't believe one can stay that way for long. Remember Revelation 3:15–16: "I know your deeds, that you are neither cold nor hot. I wish you were either one or the other! So, because you are lukewarm—neither hot nor cold—I am about to spit you out of my mouth." Hence, I had to go through what I went through—to choose sides!

On the first day of December, Shannon brought me a worksheet that had been put together by her pastor, Mark Pfeifer. He had taught that morning on weakness. The notes he prepared perfectly explained everything I had been feeling: my "bubble," the surge of strength I felt, and the hypersensitivity to the things of the Spirit. I was beginning to not despise this time spent in weakness. *There's amazing hope here.* I will share the worksheet with you just as I received it:

> Jesus said to Paul, "My strength is made perfect in weakness." What did he mean by that?

### 2 CORINTHIANS 12:7–10

> **I. Weakness in one area created strength in another.**
>
> This is true with the physical body. When one eye or ear, for instance, is weak, the other takes over. This is also true in many cases such as when people have dyslexia or children grow up in tough situations. They develop strengths that other people do not have.

## II. Usually, we don't depend on God until we have to.

Many people come to Christ initially because they have been reminded through some circumstances of their vulnerability, fragility, or mortality. Even after coming to Christ, many of us have experienced "wake-up calls" from heaven that get our attention. We become painfully aware of our weakness.

## III. Some of the greatest spiritual virtues are displayed in weakness.

Weakness brings out the best in us. There are powerful spiritual virtues that never come to the surface as long as we bluff our way through life, depending on our strengths to survive.

## IV. Great victories are often measured by the size of our weakness.

If Goliath defeats David, it does not make headlines. But when a person, sports team, or army defeats a Goliath, people take notice. Nothing is more exhilarating to a human soul than defying the odds and winning a great victory in spite of weakness.

## V. A person is most dangerous when they have nothing to lose.

Watch out for the desperate person! They are dangerous. We become an ongoing threat to the devil when we realize we have nothing to lose. We are already dead! We are intimately aware of our weaknesses and shortcomings, yet that does not discourage us. In fact, it makes us all the more aware of our need for Christ.[1]

This whole sheet impacted me, but under the third heading I noticed something particularly insightful: "There are powerful spiritual virtues that never come to the surface as long as we bluff our way through life." I realized that I myself am a recovering bluffing-my-way-through-life-er.

Even though I was a Christian and I thought I was "fine," I had a faint feeling of emptiness. I hid it well. I'm not talking about hiding it from others. I hid it from myself. Whenever it would pop up, I would swat it down and pretend (bluff) to feel fulfilled. I would use being "thankful for all I had" to avoid recognizing this complacency. But if I was truly thankful to this amazing God who had given me everything, wouldn't I, in return, long to give him *my* everything?

All along, deep down I knew there was love lacking in my marriage. I didn't want to admit it, and I had no idea how to fix it, so I pretended all was well. I bluffed. I knew I wasn't chasing God the way I should be, and my passion for him had long since slipped away, yet I held a volunteer position in our church. I bluffed again.

To *bluff* is "to pretend to be confident about an uncertain issue or to have undisclosed resources, in order to influence or deter (someone)."[2] For me, it was not so much fooling someone else, but fooling myself. Once I got real and stopped faking it, I felt liberated. Why? In exposing my own failures and weaknesses, God showed up in power like I had never known. When I relied on my own (false) strength, I had just been *bluffing* my way through life.

The last point in the worksheet, "A person is most dangerous when they have nothing to lose" was exactly how I felt now. Dangerous. This stupid devil barged into my home and tried to destroy my marriage, my *family*, the most precious people to me in the world. I felt there was nothing more he could take from me. He picked this fight, but I felt determined to finish it.

So, that day at the workshop when I announced to my group that I liked my box and had nothing I cared to change, wouldn't you agree it was odd that the very next day I would be informed that life in my box was over now, thank you very much. I was informed that I would now be a single mom and unloved, discarded by my sweetheart. The little box I loved so much was destroyed, shattered to pieces.

Here's a peek into that little box I loved so much before October 14: I had just gotten my hair done with blond high-lights and a peek-a-boo purple streak down the side. I was feeling young and pretty. I was making dinner in my newly remodeled kitchen, where I spent way too much time. It was my happy place. Chocolate chip pumpkin cookies were baking in the oven for the kids. I probably had music playing, I don't know. It was a good life. A wonderful husband. Three beautiful and rotten boys and friends as best they come.

In the evenings you could find me snuggled up on the couch with my hubs. He always gave me extra-long head rubs (my favorite) while we caught up on our shows. I felt loved and thankful. Bless my heart. I had no idea. I was about to die.

*Thank God.*

I believe God saw my life, that it was good. The fact that it was good is what kept me from desiring anything more. But I was lacking. By his grace he loved me enough that he allowed the things to happen that personally devastated me.

I recently heard someone say, "We serve a God who isn't afraid to let us suffer." The Bible is full of suffering people! This kind of suffering produces some of the strongest faith. But sadly, for many of us, just like me, if we are not faced with disaster, we are satisfied with God being and remaining only a supplement to our good lives.

But look at what suffering produces: "Not only so, but we also glory in our sufferings, because we know that suffering produces perseverance; perseverance, character; and character, hope. And hope does not put us to shame, because God's love has been poured out into our hearts through the Holy Spirit, who has been given to us" (Rom. 5:3–5).

Now that I have tasted the goodness of walking through weakness with Jesus, now that I have experienced him as comforter, provider, and judge, I am still thankful for all I have, and even more so now. But I am not satisfied to live while lacking his presence in my life. I'm not satisfied living out my routines, which were mostly self-serving, apart from him. I don't want to be lazy and stay in my comfortable life without recklessly serving where he may need me. I can say again still, I would rather return to a valley or a waiting place to be near him than to be on the highest mountaintop of victory without him.

For the previous several years, I had felt like a hamster in a spinning wheel, exerting so much energy, but accomplishing so little. In this season of recognizing my weakness, and learning total reliance on God, he has accomplished more on my behalf, working things out for my good, as I just trust in him and safely wait in his presence.

My downfall, what doomed my marriage, my biggest disaster, was not just the busyness of life, or even that I settled for the mundane. It was that in my heart I was not fully committed to God. I had wandered from my Creator. I had become satisfied apart from him. Then when my husband became satisfied apart from me, it doomed our marriage.

I had left my first love. I don't think I am alone in this. Revelation 2:3–5 warns Christians of this very common trap. "You have persevered and have endured hardships for my name, and have not grown weary. Yet I hold this against you: You have forsaken the love you had at first. Consider how far you have fallen! Repent and do the things you did at first. If you do not repent, I will come to you and remove your lampstand from its place."

How could I have been so content before? How can one truly be content outside of God's presence? Now that I have truly experienced him in this way, I know I will never be satisfied without him. I seek him every day.

# Chapter 21

# The Pursuit

*No one can come to me unless the Father who sent me draws them.*

JOHN 6:44

Looking back, I know now that God saw ahead of my situation. Before it even happened, he saw it. He goes before us. He knew that I was about to be wrecked. My lovely, stinking box was about to be blown to bits. By his unfathomable grace, he saw me and he reached out to me. *Before any of it even happened.*

Do you remember what happened in the weeks leading up to the conference in October? By his grace he had already begun giving me tastes of his sweet presence. I had started listening to worship songs in my kitchen and was so overcome with emotion I had to stop and collect myself. Then at the conference, by the night of the final worship session, I was so hungry to be filled with God, I fell, like a mad woman, onto the floor of the ballroom, soaking the carpet with tears. Why? *I was being pursued!*

His presence was so lovely and enticing. He was inviting me to indulge in those moments. He was drawing me into his presence and it was so attractive I began to want more. So I began asking God for more of himself. The Bible tells us what happens to those who want more of God. Matthew 5:6 says, "Blessed are those who hunger and thirst for righteousness, *for they will be filled*" (emphasis mine). James 4:8 says, "Come near to God and *he will come near to you*" (emphasis mine). Isaiah 55:6, "Seek the LORD *while he may be found*" (emphasis mine) What happens when we seek him? He. Will. Be. Found.

I was wooed, and in return, called out to him. While I was a pitiful hungry wretch, he came. My mind can hardly comprehend that the God of the universe, the same one who spins the planets, did this for me. He came to me in soft whispers. He beckoned me. He saw into the future. He knew I would need him, and he drew me close so that I would not be alone. It boggles my mind.

I imagine God working this process out for me, going before me, and behind. He prepared me ahead of time. He made sure I was dressed for the battle I didn't even know was coming. When I needed a rock to stand on, I was not alone. By then, I was desperate to discard my complacency and instead give myself in passionate surrender to my King.

As I write this chapter and I attempt to explain the delicate ways the Lord drew me to himself, I keep thinking of a movie I loved as a teenager, the 1996 *Romeo and Juliet* with Leonardo DiCaprio and Claire Danes, and especially the balcony scene where Romeo pursues Juliet. She is inside her bedroom. Romeo sneaks onto the grounds and climbs up the vines that wind up the wall below her window. He whispers for her. Watching this as a girl I was spellbound. The romance of it all captivated me. How exciting to be pursued!

*God did that for me.* He came searching for me. His presence surrounded me in my kitchen those nights, then again on that ballroom floor. He came gently, quietly, baiting me with his love. When we recognize and respond to the luring of a holy God, we can be saved. He draws us by his Holy Spirit, searching us out, whispering. We respond. We "open up the window" and let him in. When God pursues us, it is a pure and holy encounter, not an earthly affair between a man and a woman, so it is indescribable, but the story of the pursuing captivates me even still.

I have a friend who has not totally given her life over to God. We have talked about God often though, and she always seems to talk in future tense. She says things like, "I know I need God in my life" and "When I am ready. . . ."

Every so often she will message me. Just a few weeks ago I got one of these messages. She said, "Hey, are you going to church on Sunday? I want to come." I know that when she reaches out to me, those are seasons she can sense God is luring her in. He is pursuing her. He is whispering to her. He is drawing near to her. She has a choice now in how she will respond.

My friend still hasn't come to church with me, and usually after she has reached out to me, she stops responding altogether when I try to follow up. She closed her heart. She didn't open up the window. She was being pursued by a holy God, and her response was *not* to respond.

I only tell her story because I think that's what happens so often. God calls to us and we feel a desire to respond, but we either hesitate or we ask, *What in the world is that feeling?* And we let it pass. Remember how I described my moments of "basking" and I said it can be an embarrassing thing to do at first? The world doesn't understand. It doesn't make sense to the human eye. What kind of a person feels an invisible stirring and responds in surrender by kneeling down and giving your life away to a God you can't even see?

The kind that is being *pursued.*

As a teenager, I wanted to be Juliet (yes, I knew the outcome of the movie; I didn't care). I found her character intriguing. She was passionately in love. She was passionately loved. She was going on an adventure. Romeo and Juliet threw convention to the wind and disregarded what everyone thought about their romance. They were uninhibited, unrestrained.

That's what it takes. When God comes calling, you don't worry about what that looks like to other people. I promise you, you are about to experience a love that is more captivating than Romeo and Juliet's sad story. I cannot even begin to imagine what would have happened to me that day on October 14, had I failed to respond to God's invitation. I don't even care to think of it.

Imagine being pursued by the maker of the planets, the director of the universe, the creator of all humanity. His power is endless. We will never understand his complexity or dimensions. Yet *he* pursues *us*. He created us. He loves us. He wants to lavish grace on us. *Favor.* He desires to make us joint heirs to all he has.

I do not understand this love. But it is more fulfilling and exciting than any other love story. If you haven't yet, when you hear his whisper, and perhaps you are hearing it now, open your window and step out onto the balcony. Throw your inhibitions to the wind, and fall head over heels in love. You are his beloved, his bride.

He's coming . . . for *you*.

# Chapter 22

# Forgiveness

*I, even I, am he who blots out
your transgressions, for my own sake,
and remembers your sins no more.*

ISAIAH 43:25

From the beginning I found it absurdly easy to forgive Micah for what he had done, for I had been given an overwhelming and irrational love for him. There are, however, obviously two people involved in an affair. So inevitably I had to cope with the idea of forgiving the other woman.

For a long time, though, the need to forgive this woman did not even cross my mind. As I already explained, I really tried to be diligent to guard my thoughts. I wasn't in denial. I knew it had happened; it just didn't benefit me in any way to dwell on it. Besides, at the time I really didn't feel any personal beef toward this woman. Just common sense compelled me to feel indifferent toward her. Don't get me wrong, I *hated* what happened. But she did not make any commitment to me. She didn't know me, nor did she owe me anything. I didn't feel anger toward her. Micah was the one who had broken his word to me, not this stranger.

One day, however, I found out that this woman was divorced. And for some reason this seemingly tiny bit of knowledge shook me out of my indifference and prompted anger in me. Being divorced, surely she must have understood the hurt and pain that is associated with a failed marriage, having gone through it herself. So how could she knowingly inflict that kind of pain on me? I've never met a divorced couple who have escaped without heartbreak. Almost always, divorce is traumatic. It brings disappointment and sorrow, a pain so severe it's hard to describe. It makes everything hurt. It hurts to breathe. If kids are involved, it splits up the family. It feels like a death.

So on that day, I was filled with anger toward this woman. *So many lives are affected by this, not just yours!* I raged in my head. *How could you?* She knew about me and she knew about our children. How could she be so careless and nonchalantly willing to inflict that kind of pain and devastation on other people? I was, for the first time, offended by this woman. I felt disgusted. Repulsed. Angry.

I'm not sure if it was that day or the very next day that I reread the story of Joseph, and God did not allow those feelings of bitterness to linger long. *His grace, it's amazing.*

Of course I was familiar with Joseph's story, but now I read it with a more personal understanding, because he too had been betrayed. If you have time, go read his story now in Genesis. I'll sit right here and wait for you! If you don't have time to read it now, I will provide the CliffsNotes for you.

Joseph was his father's favorite son. After Jacob gave him a beautiful robe, his brothers became so jealous of him that they devised a plan to get rid of him. Literally. At first they wanted to kill him, but since he was indeed family, and of their own blood, they came to a compromise and threw him into a pit instead. They kept him there until a caravan of Ishmaelites passed by, at which time they sold him into slavery. (Okay. So maybe Joseph had it a tad worse than I did.)

He spent many years as a slave before being thrown into

prison, where he spent several more years, after being wrongly accused. (To say I might hold a grudge would be an understatement. Slightly.)

But God had a plan for Joseph, a plan to use his whole life and all of his experiences for good. God kept his hand on him and eventually Joseph found favor with Pharaoh. He was exalted to a high position, ruling over Egypt. In fact, there was no one with more power in all of Egypt other than the Pharaoh himself.

During this rule there was a severe famine in the land. Because God had been speaking to Joseph, he knew that the drought was coming and had prepared Egypt for it ahead of time. At Joseph's command, Egypt had stored up food, so much so, that people from other lands came in hopes that Egypt would give them some of its provisions to take back with them to feed their own people.

In this context, Joseph was reunited with the very brothers who sold him into slavery all of those years ago. They had ended his childhood, his innocence, and cost him his freedom. They now came to him as beggars. They did not recognize him.

*Pause.* I read this, humbled by this horrific story. Still just a boy, Joseph was severely betrayed and hated by the very people who should have protected him: his own brothers. His *big* brothers. *How could they?* Because of them, he was snatched from his home. He did not even get to say good-bye to his cherished father. He was led away shackled, a slave. *How could they?* All he had known, a favored, carefree, happy life, replaced with slavery, loss, and years of hardship. Oh, I think I might have had some choice words for that bunch of brothers.

But Joseph had some serious perspective. Not only does he forgive them, he helps them. Soon after this reunion, their father dies. Joseph's brothers become fearful that now with Dad gone, Joseph would let his anger loose, and they decided it would be best to beg him to just be his slaves. To that proposal Joseph responds, "Don't be afraid. Do I act for God? Don't you see, you planned evil against me but God used those same plans for my good, as you see all around you right now—life for many people" (Gen. 50:20 MSG).

What a response. What a challenge for me. These Scripture verses let me regain my own perspective. Joseph realized that the deeds of his brothers were the reason for his awesome life. God had planned everything out for his good. Not only was Joseph taken care of, but he was put in charge of taking care of others. He took care of a powerful nation who in turn took care of all the surrounding countries when a serious drought hit. He was able to provide leadership, helping a multitude of others during his time as second in command under Pharaoh's reign.

Taking a cue from Joseph, how could I be angry when good had already come out of my situation? I was experiencing a personal renaissance with my Creator. I was given a new life, one restored by God. I got to live in this closeness with the Father, and in seeing his hand and provision over my life, I was forever changed. My whole household was being affected and turned around in a new closeness with God we had never experienced before. This whole messy situation had allowed God to shine. How could I be angry when so much good had come out of this?

Joseph's brothers planned evil for him. Yet inadvertently, what they actually did was give him a platform to become great. (Remember how God loves to shine through our weakness!) This woman that wronged me didn't dig a pit and throw me into it or set out with an evil plan to destroy me. Even still, she must have known that the choices she made could have destroyed my life, my family, and my kids.

But just as God shone through Joseph's journey, God lifted me up and became great for me. I could see him at work, filling me with love for my husband, helping me to forgive. It was hard to hold a grudge when inadvertently she created a platform for God to shine and work things out for my good.

What is simply amazing to me is not only did Joseph forgive

his brothers, but he embraced them. He didn't simply forgive them and let them go. He *lavished* love on them. The red carpet was practically rolled out for them. He gave them new clothing (maybe he was making up for their jealousy over his robe all those years ago!) He gave Benjamin three hundred shekels of silver and five sets of clothes, and he sent to his father, Jacob, ten donkeys loaded with all the best Egypt had to offer, and ten more donkeys loaded with food.

I recognized this kind of forgiveness. The kind that not only lets go of the hurt, but that is able to be filled with love again without harboring bitterness. I believe this kind of forgiveness is divine, meaning it is given from our Father, not fabricated by us. It is possible only by receiving God's love and by understanding that every hardship that happens is worked together for your good and the good of those around you. I came to understand that God had not wasted a single hardship I had gone through, nor a single tear I had cried. He was using each one for his good and was wringing them out, getting the most out of every drop. He wasn't just "getting me through this." He was truly making everything beautiful. He was working all things out for my own good.

I couldn't wait to see what would happen next.

# Chapter 23

# The Golden State

*They are not just idle words for you—they are your life. By them you will live long in the land you are crossing the Jordan to possess.*

DEUTERONOMY 32:47

Finally! It was November 16, the day we were leaving to go visit California for the week. I would *never* turn down a good vacation, especially not now. Our relationship was still rocky, obviously, but we were hanging in there, sometimes by a very thin thread.

After Micah had attended college in Sacramento, his brother Blake decided to follow suit.

After completing his program, Blake married his wife, Kellie, and took a staff position at a church, so he was conveniently still living in Sacramento when we needed our emergency try-and-save-our-marriage trip. They both graciously agreed to let us stay with them for the week.

In addition to the support of Blake, Micah had a whole Christian community of "brothers" there. Among others, was his mentor, Jason Harper. He had been a spiritual father to Micah during his college years and he would be an encouragement now, to be sure.

At the time of our crisis, Micah didn't have that kind of

community in our hometown. He had friends, of course, but not men who shared godly values and principles, who challenged each other to be better men. I had noticed this area was lacking. I even reached out to some of the men in our home church at the time, urging them and hoping they would reach out and connect with Micah. Unfortunately, it didn't happen.

At least for one week, in California, Micah would have that community. I didn't know what all to expect, but it's never a bad idea to surround yourself with godly people in hard times. These people believed in prayer, in grace, and redemption. Just by placing yourself around people like that gives you an advantage.

In addition to having a support system, this would be a break from our kids. My grandma and grandpa had agreed to watch them for us. I knew I was trusting God to restore my marriage, but I was also aware that there was another woman in Micah's mind. I knew he was torn in his heart between her and me, and *how do I compete with a woman who has no kids?*

She was free to spend time pampering herself, had money to buy cute clothes (instead of spending money on kids), and probably even had time to fix her hair in the morning! Sure, she could be fun and flirty and had loads of available time to offer my husband a responsibility-free good time, *because she didn't have kids!* (You guys. I have no idea about the other woman's life. She didn't have kids, but all that other stuff was wild speculation on my part. You know this.)

Sometimes I felt like having small kids was like having a disability. Please hear me out before calling Child Protective Services. I *love* the little darling cutie pies. However, in those days I was operating in sleep deprivation mode, waking up to crying kids, dirty diapers, or trying to potty train someone in the middle of the night.

My most extensive makeup job was checking to see if I had concealed the dark circles under my eyes. My fashion statement was to accessorize with green chunks of baby food on my shoulder.

My attention was constantly diverted in several directions, making me feel like a crazy person with only interrupted, incoherent thoughts. My "me time" was often disrupted by loud bangs, and panic-inducing shrieks of "Mommeeeeeeee!"

*That week,* however, was going to be undistracted husband and wife time, with no parental responsibilities. I could be a whole, undistracted person. Needless to say, I was ridiculously excited for the trip. I had my bags packed, my hopes high. Everything was going perfectly too, until we boarded the plane.

That's right. We didn't even make it off of the runway before our hot mess began showing. Even though Micah had agreed to this trip, I knew his heart was still conflicted. He had not made his decision about our marriage and that was really difficult for me. He never really answered me directly, so I decided to feel him out and see where I stood.

If I'm being honest, I was secretly trying to see if I could make him a little jealous. A sign of jealousy would indicate to me that he did still care for me deep down, even if I couldn't get him to say it, right? Even if he left me, wouldn't it still be hard to imagine me with someone else? I should have just left well enough alone, but I pried.

I brought up Evan. I have no idea how I got there, or how it fit into our conversation, but I told him that Evan had given me his phone number that day of my run. "Seems like my old crush has a crush on me now. . . . ha ha . . . that's sort of funny, eh?"

Secretly suspecting he loved me way down deep, I was not prepared for his response. "Shauna, if you want to be with this guy, go do it. I think it would be a good thing." He did not say it to be mean, nor to be kind. Just robotic. If I was hoping for some fierceness to kick in, some passion that had been repressed, any feelings that remained toward me at all, it was crushed with those words.

*What in the world are we doing on this plane?* My face flushed a hot pink, as the impact of his words settled in my stomach in a nauseated pit. I turned my face toward the window and demanded the tears stay inside. They did not listen.

Micah saw. "I'm sorry," He whispered. "I don't want to feel that way. I don't. I just feel fine with you moving on. I know there is something wrong with me, because I shouldn't feel that way." Then he added, sincerely again, "I'm sorry."

Surprisingly, somehow that did make me feel better. I was praying for a breakthrough. He *wants* to feel attracted to me. That's a start. That's better than last week, right? I knew all along this would not be an easy journey. And here it was, not being easy. This was no surprise.

He extended his arm across the seat and turned his hand over. I took it. We held hands as the tears rebelliously rolled down my face. The plane jolted and began its fast incline off the runway.

I rested my head on the seat back and looked back out the window, feeling defeated, yet somehow, also amused. *Look at us. What a mess. If this works out, it's going to make one heck of a story.*

We spent the first day of our visit in San Francisco. I had been so looking forward to this day, but in reality, it was hard. It was hard to re-trace steps we took ten years ago holding a man's hand who couldn't care less if I went and married someone else. It was hard bearing this still-new information that my husband had been with someone else. The pain was still tender, and our marriage so very precarious.

But I had been learning to put my trust in God, not in people. That included Micah. God had gotten me this far.

Once we got to Blake and Kellie's house, Kellie pulled me aside and told me that the church was having a night of worship that evening. It was by sheer coincidence, she said, as they usually didn't have Sunday night services at the time. It was like hearing they had a cure for a disease I had. *Worship was my salve.* I knew Micah would want to go and see all of his people, so I was excited to have him there, standing beside me for an evening in God's presence.

As Shannon had said in the beginning, if Micah and I both chased after God and sought him, our marriage would naturally fall into alignment as a result. So I needn't worry if he didn't like me. That was only a small problem for God, surely. He raised people from the dead, after all. Surely He could make my husband like me again.

What I needed was for my husband to meet with God face-to-face. Worship is such a great opportunity to meet with him and that night of worship truly was impacting. I even got to see Micah slip his hand up to God, in surrender. What hope that brought me!

The next night, we met with a man named Russell. He used to be in our youth group when we first got married and Micah was a youth pastor fresh out of Bible college. We met him after dark, at a deep dish pizza place nestled in the heart of downtown Sacramento and we were seated in a cozy little booth. Russell sat across from us and asked us how we were doing. So we told him. After listening to what brought us back to Cali, he thanked us for our honesty.

Then he said to Micah, "I don't know how you measure success, or your worth in life. I don't know if you measure your value by how successful you are in your career, or by some other way. I know you might feel like a failure right now. But let me tell you, I owe a lot of my success to you. You may not realize the impact you've made on people, but for me personally, that impact was huge. You poured into me without wanting anything in return. You just cared about me, took the time to invest in me, and because of that, I am where I am today, in large part because of you."

For the first time, I saw Micah feeling. For the first time in our ten years of marriage, I saw him cry. He sat across the dimly lit pizza booth listening to a now grown man whom he admired speak truth to him.

Maybe for the first time we realized the impact our marriage had on others. We were in so deep it seemed like it was just our problem, effecting only ourselves and our kids. But people we have sewn into over the years surely would feel some sort of impact from this. It was a sobering moment for us both. That conversation with Russell was a turning point for Micah.

That Wednesday was my birthday. I woke up to glorious quiet. Micah had already gone downstairs by the time I got going. He said, "I know it's your birthday, but Blake needs some help at the church this morning. Would it be okay if I help him out for a little bit and when I get back I'll take you out for your birthday?" I readily agreed and was excited to have a whole morning in peace and quiet to myself!

I plopped on the sofa with my Bible and a yellow marker, anxious to spend my birthday morning in God's Word. *Maybe God has something to give me for my birthday too.* I opened up the Word to discover that God's birthday presents really are the best.

"Now what I am commanding you today is not too difficult for you or beyond your reach. It is not up in heaven, so that you have to ask, 'Who will ascend into heaven to get it and proclaim it to us so we may obey it?' Nor is it beyond the sea, so that you have to ask, 'Who will cross the sea to get it and proclaim it to us so we may observe it?' No, the word is very near you; it is in your mouth and in your heart so you may obey it" (Deut. 30:11–14).

God had asked me to do something unthinkably hard. It had been a little over a month since he gave me the Love Filter to follow. I had set off to follow him on this path he so graciously invited me to go on with him. My days looked something like this: obedience, panic, hope, terrifying fear, then peace, obedience again, and so forth, like steady waves all day. It was a roller coaster of the divine versus earthly weakness and instability.

I wanted my husband back. Literally following the Love Filter in God's Word seemed impossible, unattainable. There were days I felt too incompetent to walk in that kind of obedience. The fear of failure threatened to paralyze hope. This was hard. But not too hard. Did you see that verse? "What I am commanding you today is not too difficult for you or beyond your reach."

If the Lord tells you on your birthday that what he's asked you to do is difficult, *but not too difficult,* you are likely to believe him. I did. Furthermore, Deuteronomy 32:47 reads, "They are not just idle words for you—they are your life. By them you will live long in the land you are crossing the Jordan to possess."

These encouraging verses I was finding were not just ancient texts, sometimes familiar but mostly forgotten. For me, *they are life. They offered life.* They changed my life. They change me now. How unexpected that this time spent in Scripture became one of the highlights of our trip for me.

On the last day in California, we spent a large amount of time at the beach. One thing I love about San Francisco is that surrounding the busy Bay Area, are stunning beaches, tucked away in seemingly forgotten places. Some with abandoned lighthouses or bridges, historic and cultural finds that are unique to the area. Many of these places hide behind giant cliffs made of rock. They are giant coves, peaceful retreats from the loud city. So beautifully tucked away are these secret places, you feel like you might be trespassing, but the view is free for the taking!

We spent the afternoon at one of these beaches. It was November, so a bit too chilly for me to swim. As we walked along the shore, the sun was brilliant. Micah decided it would be great to run a few miles on the sand, so I walked alone along the pebble-laced shore and prayed. I thought of 1 Samuel 7:12, "Then Samuel took a stone. . . . He named it Ebenezer, saying, 'Thus far the LORD has helped us.'"

I had the idea to pick out a stone from the beach that day, so that if God did a miracle, and our marriage was restored, I could have it as my own memorial to remember that day I spent in the trenches. I didn't know what my life would look like when we returned home. But at least for now, at this spot mid-journey I could say, "This far, the Lord has helped me."

Our week had come to an end and we were checking our luggage at the airport. My bag was just a few pounds over the weight limit. It always seems a bit humiliating when this happens and you have to open bags full of your personal things and move them into different bags to get it all to weigh in correctly.

As I rummaged through my pack, I felt the blood rush to my face in embarrassment. *My Ebenezer stone.* Here in the busy terminal, surrounded by people, it just looked like a silly, heavy rock that was causing a scene at the airport. I tried to discard it quickly without attracting attention from other travelers who may be wondering, *Why is she carrying around a rock?* I was going to stick it in a nearby potted plant when Micah realized what I was doing. He picked up the rock and handed it back to me and said, "No. Take your stone. We'll get rid of something else."

# Chapter 24

# Spiritual Warfare

*Be sober-minded; be watchful. Your adversary the
devil prowls around like a roaring lion, seeking
someone to devour.*

1 PETER 5:8 ESV

Iknew I couldn't write a book about God saving my marriage
without including a chapter on spiritual warfare. To imply that
it wasn't a real and significant part of this journey would be dis-
honest and a gross disservice to the reader. This has been one of
the last chapters that I have written because quite honestly, I have
been putting it off. I hesitate to write about it because so many
Christians I know tend to get squeamish when you start talking
about demonic activity in spiritual warfare. Still, it was a real part
of our struggle.

There are those who err on either side of this camp. Those
giving Satan too much credit for their own bad choices and those
who refuse to believe that demons and powers and authorities of
darkness even exist at all. I am not attempting to take sides on this
debate in any way or promote a certain ideology. I just simply can't
accurately share my story without including what happened along
the way, and spiritual warfare played a big part. I've never even

studied theology on this subject, so I ask for grace as I do my best to find the right words to articulate what we experienced.

In our marriage crisis, a lot of stuff was going on behind the scenes (as there usually is). Just as God was behind the scenes working for us on our behalf, so also the enemy lurked and schemed and instructed his army to derail us from our course. I felt like at the beginning of it all, God told me that this whole situation wasn't even about me and that it went beyond me fighting for our marriage. I don't know how to explain the urgency I felt. I felt that Micah had a target on his back and that he was under a direct spiritual attack.

It actually seemed he had that target on his back for a long time, even after surviving his rocky childhood. When we were first married, we lived in northern California. We got pregnant shortly after and decided to move back to our home state of Ohio to be closer to our family. We were barely out of Cali, on our way home, when Micah was in a terrible accident.

I was following his truck in my car when I noticed he swerved left of center. I pulled up beside him to see if he was okay and he smiled and said he was just sleepy as we had left really early in the morning to beat traffic. He turned up his radio, rolled down the windows, and assured me he was fine. He said that we would stop in Reno, only twenty minutes away.

The next time he swerved left of center, he didn't catch himself. He fell asleep at the wheel. He was barreling full-speed ahead, close to sixty miles per hour, into the forest and smashed head-on into a tree. My heart froze. My fingers gripped my steering wheel as I helplessly watched from behind. I still remember thinking in that moment, *He's dead. I'm pregnant and my husband is dead.*

The accident looked horrific. I remember bracing myself as I crossed the road for what I would find when I went over to the truck. The whole front end was smashed. It more or less looked like the truck had wrapped itself around the tree. I braced myself for the worst. I got to the window and Micah was looking at me.

At first I was terrified. *Why are his eyes open, looking at me?* Then it hit me: *he's alive!* I remember standing there beside the wreckage and throwing both arms up in the air and shouting praises to God. Pretty sure I did a little dance too.

Micah had a scrape on his knee. *A scrape.* His big leather flip-flop was stuck because the truck had mangled itself around it, yet his foot was not crushed. All the glass was busted out except the very back window behind his head. Someone from the highway had called a rescue squad. The workers could not deny the miracle. Nor did I.

Since we were moving across the country, the bed of the pickup was full of our boxes. We pulled out pots and pans that had been disfigured. Yet Micah walked away from that horrific accident with nothing hurt but his pride.

The rescuers pointed out another miracle. We were right outside of Reno in the mountains. At the moment Micah fell asleep we had been winding up a cliff. These steep mountains are so common in that area, there are not even guard rails—just a drop off the side of the mountain.

The first responders explained to us that in most accidents that happen as a result of someone falling asleep, the driver almost always veers off to the right, because most people are right-handed. But Micah is left-handed so he veered off into the forest. I couldn't get out of my mind that had he veered to the right, I would have had to helplessly watch as he drove right off the edge of the cliff.

After the accident, we stayed in a hotel before continuing our road trip. Micah confided to me that the night before, he did not sleep well because he had a dream that a demon was trying to kill him. Being married to Micah, and knowing his story, "a demon trying to kill him" was not that far-fetched.

This man has survived more obstacles than almost anyone else I knew. The people who knew about Micah's childhood home life always talked about what an overcomer he was, using him as an example of someone who had bettered himself with none of the advantages that most people have. People sang his praises. I was one of them.

Throughout our marriage, I never heard him say a harsh word about anyone. He didn't express anger at his circumstances, nor hold on to grudges. He seemed to effortlessly move on. He was kind to the people who wronged him. He was fast to point out the best qualities in people when I had a tendency to let their issues obstruct my view. His character and his ability to do this always amazed me.

I've always thought he had such an incredible testimony and I was puzzled that he never shared it. He rarely even talked about it, even if asked direct questions. This started making sense to me as we moved on in our process of healing. As a little boy he had perfected the skill of building up walls to escape all the horrors of that life. As he built up walls, he would learn to escape to a place where he would feel nothing.

To avoid feelings of failure, rejection, and sadness, he retreated into survival mode. I suspect he went back to that place of building up walls after disappointment had crept into our marriage. Eventually, he stopped hoping for more, because he had already perfected the skill of not being disappointed or hurt.

The problem with building the walls, as I recently heard him explain, is that they do in fact protect you from all the negative feelings. They also, however, keep you from experiencing the good things, like the ability to feel *at all*. This little skill could render someone unable to receive the love that is right in front of them. In that state, he had approached me with "I feel nothing for you." *He was pinning all of that on me!*

One night, in a rare moment of open communication, we were lying in bed and he said, "I don't understand why you are fighting so hard for this."

I abruptly responded, "Then you've never loved anyone."

It just slipped out. I didn't even have time to think about what I was saying. It wasn't harsh, only honest. He pondered what I said, and made the noise, "Hmm." But it wasn't a sarcastic or offended sound. I think in that moment, we both realized that my statement was true. I think he had loved me as much as he could up to that moment. It was truly amazing he had loved me to any measure at all living with all of his walls in place.

During the course of our marriage, I didn't want to become resentful to him for not having the life or marriage we had once dreamed of. So I shoved my expectations and those dreams under the rug. I thought this was a sacrifice of love on my part, to not dwell on the negative, and just be thankful for the things we did have. But what I failed to know was that our collective passiveness was killing Micah.

I realize now that accepting his apathy was not loving at all. I had no faith in God to change our situation and I had no faith in my husband to accomplish his dreams. In the past, I had felt shot down when I would try and encourage him, so I simply gave up. When I got frustrated, I would blame his childhood. And I labeled it "love." (It is not my proudest moment admitting that, and certainly will not be winning any wife-of-the-year awards with that kind of love.) I see now how wrong this was, since it violates the Love Filter. *Love* never gives up. *Love* always hopes for the best.

By the time he set out to do this extramarital act, he was desperate to feel something, *anything*. Before he started to resent me, he must have resented God first. He had been called to serve God with his life and he had abandoned that calling. I had seen the indifference Micah had toward God in recent years, but I didn't know what to do about it. So I did nothing. *I did nothing!* Perhaps I could have hit my knees and interceded on his behalf. But it didn't bother me too much when he abandoned God. It only became real when he abandoned me. *God, I'm so sorry . . .*

By the time I woke up, I was in the midst of a full-fledged

battle. That's why I keep referring to those days in October and early November, before restoration began, as *in the trenches*. What I came to understand was that the enemy had slipped his foot in. And not during the course of all of this. It was the *cause* of all of this. I became convinced that the words Micah had spoken to me were not true. Lies had been planted in his mind by the enemy and they had taken root until Micah believed them.

How could he feel that he could walk out of our home, away from our family, and I would be "okay" with this? He said I would be better off finding someone "I deserve," and the kids would be better off without him too. He would still be in town and close by, after all, if we needed anything. Why was I being so dramatic? *How could he think this was no big deal?* How could he give us up? How could he feel that he had nothing to lose? How was his mind so warped that he could justify this? Without question, I knew in my heart that I was up against something greater than Micah's feelings.

I am not saying these things to absolve him from responsibility of the poor choices that he made to lead us to this point. We are responsible for our own actions, certainly. I am not one to buy into, "The devil made me do it." God always provides a way of escape for us. However, 1 Peter 5:8 gives us a clear warning: "Be sober-minded; be watchful. Your adversary the devil prowls around like a roaring lion, seeking someone to devour."

The first thing that alerted me of a demonic presence in our home happened while I was sleeping in our basement. Since Micah worked nights, he slept in the basement during the day so the noise of the kids wouldn't disturb him. I rarely slept down there because it was two stories away from the kids' rooms, which were on the second story of our home. That night, however, Micah was upstairs with the kids, and for a reason I don't remember, I retired to the basement. We had already returned home from our California trip, and things had really started to look up for us. At that point, Micah and I were at the stage in our relationship where Micah had made a decision to be with me and was sincerely trying to make things right. I had also noticed Micah had begun pursuing God again.

As I drifted to sleep that night, my thoughts were bombarded with Bible verses. This happened very often during my battle. It was not unusual for me to dwell on Scripture as I woke up and as I was falling asleep. That night, however, the Scriptures that came to me were the ones that talk about not associating yourself with fornicators and those who commit adultery (for example, 1 Corinthians 5:11). I can't even remember what all the verses were specifically, but I remember fragments from verses swirling through my head, phrases like, "cutting off the wicked person" and "purging them from your home," and words like "unclean." It seemed to be a warning. The verses pounded in my head.

At first I thought God was speaking to me again. He often spoke to me in the quiet of the night. This was *Scripture* after all! *Is God giving me a warning?* I began to panic. I thought, "Oh no, Micah must be going to make another bad choice and God is getting me ready, this time my instructions will be to cut him off!" I thought about everything we had been through to get to this point and how truly happy I was to have his heart returning to me. I didn't want to lose him! I didn't want to go through all of this again!

I became anxious and I realized I felt sick. I had a giant pit in my stomach. I felt nervous and scared. Just the thought of cutting Micah off or making him leave our home made me feel nauseated. But I realized it didn't make sense for God to take me through all of this, finally start to see breakthrough, and all of a sudden, "Nope! Never mind! Cut him out!"

Looking back I can see that the verses that swirled in my brain were broken up, pieced together, out of context, random, and distorted. I realized all the other times when God would speak a word to me, it was followed by peace. Always. Even when he told me to do something extremely difficult and challenging, there was peace. It was never followed by panic or fear. Right then, I felt a dark presence right above me and I knew it was a spiritual being speaking these things to me, but it was not God. By now God's presence was familiar to me. This one was not.

I thought about how confused I had become just in the few moments of hearing those whisperings. I imagined how confused I might be if I heard things being whispered to me all the time! What if I heard them every night? I thought of Micah. Now that I had identified an outsider was present, I wondered if he was tormenting Micah constantly as he slept? No wonder he seemed so confused!

After I had fallen asleep, I woke up at some point in the night after having a terribly sexually explicit dream. The man in the dream was not my husband, but I knew him. What in the world was going on here? For months I had been so enamored by love and attraction for my husband, more than I ever had before. Why in the world would these thoughts be provoking me now as I slept?

It was then I remembered the verses that had been going through my mind as I fell asleep and how awful I had felt about the idea of having to cut Micah off if God required that of me. I realized I had become a target. Whatever demon had been speaking lies to Micah was now pointing its arrows in my direction. I became offended by this attack. I thought, *How dare you come into my home and speak to my husband and then attempt to speak to me!*

In some odd way I felt relief, relief that a problem had been located. You can't fix a problem you don't know is there. I also felt empathy. After having had those moments of sheer confusion, and understanding how crafty and manipulative the enemy is, I had a greater understanding of what Micah may have been up against. I could at least now comprehend how all this may have happened.

The demon started off subtly, tricky, feeding innocent thoughts into my mind. Each moment that thought was entertained, it grew stronger and stronger. (We have a saying in our house now, if one of us feels offended, angry, or even just down in the dumps, we say,

"You better lock that up!" It's our reminder to each other to always be on guard and not to entertain thoughts that go against what we know God would have for us.)

The thought of Micah being targeted every night as he slept actually explained a lot! During the whole battle I kept thinking he was acting like a man in torment. I even explained it that way to Aunt Jan and Shannon because he just seemed so torn. I could see it in his eyes. I could see it on his face. I could sense it in my spirit, but I had no "proof." Could that be why, I wondered, our relationship had been so up and down and unstable? One minute he wanted to do one thing and the next, another. Was this the cause of my emotional whiplash? Now I was ready to end this.

I contacted my Aaron and Hur about what had happened and what I sensed in the basement. They were both familiar with spiritual warfare and Shannon told me not to be frightened, that God's blessing is stronger than any curse. (But she came by my house that night and prayed for me anyway, even though it was in the middle of the night, because she is awesome! Seriously, everyone needs a Shannon or an Aunt Jan. If you don't have one, be one for someone else. God will reward your labors, I'm sure!)

Within the next few days, we called a team meeting. Shannon, John, and Micah's dad, Bill, came over and we sat in the living room and talked. I explained that I never sensed anything in any other part of the house except for in the basement. That led us into a conversation about how some demons are territorial, meaning that they latch on to a certain place and stay there. Other demons are generational, meaning they latch on to certain family lines, attacking each generation with the same tricks. In Christian circles these are referred to as "generational curses."

Generational curses are when someone's sons and daughters (lineage lines) are attacked with the same spiritual bondage as their fathers (or mothers). It can last whole lines of generations, for decades—probably centuries—if not broken. Generational curses can be anger issues, drug or alcohol addictions, divorce, adultery, depression, et cetera. Some of these things are learned behaviors, to be sure. But just as God strategically moves on our behalf to save us, so the enemy has strategic moves as well, plans for our destruction. Generational curses are just a tactic he uses.

I was reminded again of what Shannon had said to Micah while giving him that haircut a few weeks before. She suggested that the trick the enemy used on their mother was convincing her she had nothing to lose, but ultimately she lost everything. Likewise, Micah's mother was not raised by her own parents. Her mother gave her up and she was raised by her grandparents. There was definitely an ongoing pattern that seemed to show true to what Shannon was saying. This seemed to be a generational curse that was present in his family lines. And who knows about the generations before that?

I thought again about his mother. The addiction left her all but handicapped. The need for supplying her addiction had caused a very self-absorbed existence. Her own children had to distance themselves from her as she often left a messy trail behind her that was hard not to get tangled up in. The end of her life was so sad, when at one time she had everything to live for. And she gave it all away. The outcome of believing that lie had been a very lonely life.

*Is this how Satan would have every one of us?* That is what he's fighting so hard for. Total loss. Total destruction. Remember 1 Peter 5:8 uses the word, "devour." That means "to swallow or eat up hungrily, voraciously, or ravenously." [1]

Micah's mom willingly gave up everything. Why? *Her problem was that the enemy tricked her into thinking she had nothing to lose.* I thought of the demon that hovered over me in the basement that had been speaking to Micah all that time. I wondered if that was the same demon that's been following and harassing this family for years. I instantly suspected it was. It had to be generational. It's such a common strategy the enemy uses, his go-to move. It was as if that thing hopped off of the back of one family member and set up camp waiting to attack, looking for a way into the new generation.

I kept thinking the enemy was going through a whole lot of trouble to destroy this man, my husband. I began to recognize and understand the calling on Micah's life. God was showing miracle upon miracle to change us. *Why?* I decided God must have something huge in store. He must love him so very much. And no demons nor any other principality could stand in the way of God's power or his plan.

Shannon, John, Bill, Micah, and I finally headed downstairs into the basement. Bill took over with calm authority. He said, "Here's what we're gonna do. We are going to speak the name of Jesus." He said that in his past when he had to get rid of a demonic presence from his own space, the name of Jesus was the only thing that worked.

Relief. *Okay. Perfect. Sounds good to me. I am familiar with that name!*

John had been walking around the basement as we talked. He had wandered into the adjoining room. Suddenly he became very stern and he looked at me and pointed to the chalkboard wall that we had painted for the kids a few years before. "Who wrote this?" he demanded.

In the mess of the kid's scribbles was hidden what appeared to be three stars with circles around them, all lined up together. Drawn with the circles around them they very eerily resembled the Wiccan pentagram. As soon as I saw what he was pointing to, I got chills from the top of my head to the bottom of my toes. I remembered the day that was written with chalk on the wall. I didn't think anything about it at the time. It was written by Micah's mother.

She had come over for a visit (which was very rare) and was playing a "game" in the basement with Josiah. I always had a weird feeling when she was around, so I stayed close and monitored her time with my kids. I remember the stars that were written on the wall had been her way of "keeping score" in the game. In the moment John pointed it out, there was no way he could have known who wrote that.

Yet he instructed, having no context at all, "This writing is demonic and it needs to come down." John had me wet a washcloth and cleaned every bit of chalk from the wall. As he did, he prayed for a clean slate. We prayed and anointed the doors and windows. After that, Bill laid hands on each of us and anointed and prayed over us.

As he prayed over Micah, he told him that God had a plan for his life. He then affirmed him, "Do not wait to allow God to use you until this recent failure is a good and safe distance into the past. That would be our tendency, to feel like we have failed God and we are not good enough to be used anymore, at least until we feel like we have somehow earned being good enough again. We are never good enough, but he uses us anyway. When we give our lives to God, we no longer belong to ourselves anymore. He uses us because we are his. Because we told him we are his."

As they chatted, Micah went over to the bookshelf and picked up a book. It was *The Screwtape Letters* by C. S. Lewis. When he opened up the book, two pictures fell out—pictures I had taken of Micah's accident, that day near Reno where his truck had smashed into the trees. The pictures revealed just how narrowly he had escaped death that day. And now today, once again, God had saved him.

After the demon was identified and cast out, things started progressing at a faster pace for us. The confusion that was hidden behind Micah's eyes was gone after that. Although he had honestly been working on our marriage before that happened, I could see now that he believed restoration in our marriage was possible. And it was a whole lot easier! Any hesitation he seemed to have before was now gone. Any reluctance or self-doubt he had seemed to vanish also.

God continued working in Micah. He began laying his hands on me and the kids and blessing us before we went to sleep. He began searching for God more fiercely. The apathy and numbness he had suffered before were gone and replaced with new life. He was set free.

In case I haven't clarified this enough, I am not an expert on the topic of spiritual warfare. But I do have a theory on why that crafty demon was hiding in our basement. I never had any problems anywhere else in the house. The only encounters I had with it were down there. I wondered why?

Remember how I said that when Micah decided to leave me, I became like an addict after God's presence? I was in a constant state of seeking him, in communion with him. I had praise and worship music on *all the time*. His praise was being lifted up in our home. Light cannot mix with darkness. I believe God's powerful presence had reduced that thing to hiding in a corner of the basement. Poor thing. He didn't stand a chance.

If this whole story has made you squeamish and you just can't wrap your head around believing it, I can imagine what you might be thinking: *Wow. This woman's husband tells her he wants to leave her and she decides it's more likely he is possessed by a demon than just not being attracted to her!*

Well, obviously. How could he not be attracted to me? Haven't you seen my Facebook selfies?

Oh, come now. I kid.

# Chapter 25

# A Heart of Flesh

*I will give you a new heart and put a new spirit in*
*you; I will remove from you your heart of stone and*
*give you a heart of flesh.*
EZEKIEL 36:26

Our relationship had already hit so many new milestones in the short amount of time we had spent in the restoration process. Each milestone was cause for renewed hope. Even still, I was cautious at first. Who knew what each passing month would hold? Micah had still not given me my ring back, and as far as I knew, that meant he still hadn't made up his mind about us, completely and for sure. We had been through a lot in a very short amount of time. I knew that without God changing both our hearts, our marriage would never be fully restored.

As I've mentioned before, we had high moments and low ones. The high ones provided such hope whereas the low ones seemed to completely derail all the progress we'd made. I had stopped praying early on for our marriage and was only praying that God would restore Micah's first love and draw him back unto himself.

Thanksgiving was uneventful. I was just happy to be at Thanksgiving with him at his grandma's house for family dinner that year instead of some new woman taking my spot! By Christmas, our relationship was in a much better place as God continued to work in both of our hearts. You can see this reflected by peeking into my journal entry from Christmas morning:

It's 9:30 a.m. Christmas morning. This has already by far been the best Christmas. I am so thankful for sharing this Christmas with my husband and our kids. Shannon said the other day that when God restores something, he doesn't just bring it back to the way that it was. He restores it to its original intent.

For Christmas, I am reflecting and living in a restored passion personally and in my marriage. I know if I would read back to these first chapters, it would take me back to that faraway place where my heart was breaking and hope seemed lost. In reality, it was only a few short months ago, truly. But it is far removed from me.

Last night we brought the kids and Rebecca to my mom's house to spend the night for Christmas Eve. After everyone went to bed, Micah and I stayed up. We did our Chase Bible study "homework" from Shannon and John. Micah has been studying the books of Samuel on his own and was sharing about what he's been reading and shared with me some pretty amazing insights about those Scripture passages I had never thought about before. He had a passion in his eyes and his voice that made it evident God had been speaking to him.

There was something sacred about staying up with him on Christmas Eve in the quiet of my parents' house. It is very clear to me that God's hand is working and stirring up gifts that have long laid dormant. He is sparking in Micah a new-found passion for his Word, and he has been given a gift to explain the Bible in a way that is thought-provoking and contagious.

He also was listening to old songs from around the time we started dating. As one of the songs played, I asked him to dance with me. He was being so thoughtful and tender, and the lights were all off except for the Christmas tree. We danced in the living room of my parents' house, and to me it was magical.

I can't get enough of his kisses on my hair and on my face, or his hands tightly pressing on my back or his hugs around my shoulders. I can't get enough of taking him in and pressing my face into his chest or taking in his smell.

It feels safe there and I am over the moon. He is leading and I am following him. I am lost in his sweet presence. Was this God's intent all along?

I had an abundance of God's blessings poured out on me in the few months of crisis while pursuing God. I saw his faithfulness and his wisdom working in my life, sustaining me and surrounding me with his tangible presence, his provision. His Word and passion being made alive again in me.

But to have his restoration power that had been avidly working in my marriage, and changing my relationship with my husband to an extent we never even had before was just extra, and showing off.

I looked up a text message I had received from Aunt Jan in November. The context is that she was frustrated that I was on this "roller-coaster" ride that I did not sign up for. That at the time, with each step forward, I seemed to be shoved two steps back. I would be given an ounce of hope one day only to have it yanked away a moment later. This is the text from Aunt Jan:

"I think this is a *fair prayer* for you—I pray that you're not on the Roller Coaster, the Scrambler, the Whip, the Twister, or the Death Drop—and that the Strongman doesn't pound you with all his might . . . but that you get to see exhibits that people have worked on, eat cotton candy and candied apples, ride the Merry Go Round, laugh in the Fun House, go through the Tunnel of Love, and win the Prize!!!"

At the time, I couldn't see it. I was in a mess, my world in a thousand little pieces. But I believed God. I am thanking him relentlessly for giving me the strength I needed not to give up before being awarded such an immense blessing. Being in the midst of God's nearness in brokenness, being sustained by his great provision when I was at a complete loss, and now seeing his restorative power alive and at work in my marriage is beyond anything I deserve. I am thankful. He is showing off. And I am loving it.

In February, Capitol Christian Center, our home church in Sacramento, was planning a massive youth conference called MyCity. Micah's brother Blake was instrumental in the conference planning and preparations. He asked Micah if he would like to come back and help serve for the week.

We decided Micah would go to Sacramento by himself this time. I stayed home with the kids. I had already seen God do so much, but I knew he was *in process*. God was still working on him. The conference was to be a big event. Hillsong Young and Free was on the roster to lead worship and they were bringing in several speakers. They would need lots of extra hands to pull off such a big weekend.

I can't explain how I knew this, but *I just knew* that God was going to do a mighty work in Micah's heart that weekend. I was excited for him that he was getting to go, but also a bit bummed I wouldn't be there to see it. So I prayed, "God, help me to get to see a moment of change in his life. When you speak to him, I want to see it." I had prayed so much and hoped so much, and I got to see glimpses, but I hated to miss any of it.

Micah slept in Blake's office at the church that week, staying up late those few nights leading up to the conference. Since he was staying at the church and his purpose was to help with conference prep, he was spending a lot of time with the interns. During lunch one day, right in the middle of the lunchroom, a few interns and a staff pastor asked if they could lay hands on Micah and pray over him. Those men had no idea about our situation, how much he really needed that encouragement, and that I was back home in Ohio praying for my husband to have a God-encounter. Just another example of people being used by God simply by being obedient and reaching out to someone.

When the evening service was starting, I got a text from Micah telling me that I could live stream the message online. Carl Lentz, lead pastor from Hillsong New York, was speaking that night. From the view of the camera, I couldn't see all of the audience, which appeared to be a few thousand or more. Oddly enough, I found Micah. Being Blake's brother, he got some special privileges and I saw him sitting to the side of the stage which looked like a "reserved" seating section. There was only a handful of people sitting in the section that night.

Mid-message, Pastor Lentz stopped what he was saying, turned to that section, and said, "God just gave me a word for someone over here right now." He locked eyes with Micah and pointed his way, "God says to tell you, *see it through.*"

That was it. Simple. Amazing. From my couch in Ohio I watched Pastor Carl Lentz stop his message, point his finger, and deliver a word directly to my husband. Shortly after this, the live stream disconnected. I couldn't believe it. Maybe that's not really what I just saw? Maybe he wasn't really looking at Micah? It was a weird camera angle, and there were so many people.

Micah had started following Pastor Lentz recently by listening to him speak online and had grown quickly to respect his teaching and message. For this reason, I knew he would receive that message from him and it would really mean a lot coming from this man. But perhaps I was making something out of nothing? And *see it through*? Did that even mean anything to Micah?

I stayed up late and waited for Micah's phone call. He called me after he got back to Blake's office a few hours later. His voice was soft and hoarse. He sobbed on the phone with me. The man had been *wrecked* by God that night. He was at a loss in response to the grace, redemption, and provision that was being laid out before him in so many different ways. The Lord had done a great work, softening a heart that had been hardened before.

When Micah came home, this softening continued. Blake had told him to look up Sermon Jams by Judah Smith, and he found one titled, "Jesus is Loving Barabbas." (If you have a few minutes, give it a quick listen for an outstanding message on unworthiness and grace. I'll wait right here.)

Micah added this to his running mix and would listen to it over and over while he ran. He was filling himself with the Word of God, just as I had done. Everywhere he turned he was faced with grace and the story of redemption. We began sharing with each other the things God was doing in us separately. In that season I was given the ability to extend grace in a supernatural way. Perhaps the hardest challenge, though, was Micah's.

Accepting it.

# Chapter 26

# *Intimacy*

*As the Father has loved me, so have I loved you. Now remain in my love.*

JOHN 15:9

My middle son, Gabe, went through a phase for a few years where he loved when I read stories to him. *The Three Little Pigs*, *Goldilocks and the Three Bears*, and *The Boy Who Cried Wolf* were among his favorites. He loves make-believe. And he has a wild imagination! He didn't want to grow up. He wanted to sit on my lap and pretend with me. He gives the best hugs and kisses and always said the sweetest little things. He was sent to speech classes at age four because he was still pronouncing words like a baby. He would say, "Mommy, I wub you!" He was saying it wrong, but it was so darn cute!

I think one of the reasons I love that preschool age so much is because it is so intimate. Time spent reading, finger painting, storytelling, and playing pretend. And the cuddling, oh my heart! These are all things we do together. Preschoolers are big enough to discover adventure and have their own personalities, which is so fun, but they still depend largely on mom and dad. It's a close and personal stage.

Matthew 18:3 says, "Truly I tell you, unless you change and become like little children, you will never enter the kingdom of heaven." Intimacy in relationships is important. Just like my marriage needed intimacy to survive, we also must find intimacy in Christ, just like a child. We cannot skip this crucial step.

The restoration that took place in our marriage was a process. My heart was for my husband completely, but the recovery was delicate at first. I have shared that Micah was trying to work on our marriage before his heart was really in it, which was obviously difficult for me. No wife wants her husband's obligations without his love. As God ministered to his heart and healed him of past hurts and began giving him the ability to love, I treaded lightly. God had required me at the very beginning to be patient. (Patience—*my nemesis!*)

As Micah began opening up his heart to me, I proceeded with caution. At first he was wishy-washy. He wanted me, then he didn't want me. Some days were harder than others as I didn't know who I would get when he woke up—the one who wanted me, or the one who didn't.

Just as God had assured me in the beginning, eventually the days where he didn't want me did not return. There came a point where God's love had trumped every doubt and uncertainty, and the love in Micah's heart was solidified and made whole. There came a point of security in our marriage again. In fact, I have referred to our marriage in two parts. "The first marriage" and the "second marriage." We never divorced, but the difference between the two marriages is night and day. Our marriage is still not perfect, of course, but I never imagined I'd have the positive, productive, loving relationship that I enjoy with my husband today.

Yet during those initial weeks and months after restoration first began, I needed extra reassurance. I needed extra attention. After everything that had happened and all the uncertainty that was displayed, if Micah wanted me to feel secure in his love again there were a few things I needed. I needed date nights, hand-holding, long kisses, heart-to-heart talks, uninterrupted Micah time. I needed intimacy.

When I got those things, I didn't feel the need to ask the questions that nagged at me on the inside in those days. *Do you want me? Are you going to stay with me? Are you going to leave me?*

The work God was doing in Micah's heart was blaring and evident. He had never been that expressive with his affections for me in our first marriage. He was uncomfortable with it in the past and wasn't one to express his feelings in any of those ways. In our new and restored marriage it seemed to come naturally.

Now when he would wake up or come home, he would take me in his arms and kiss my forehead. He would grab my hand and pull me to the couch and ask me about my day. Really, for the first time in our marriage, I felt prioritized and valued. I began to believe his words when he told me that he loved me. (And yes, my love languages are physical touch and quality time so someone else's healing may look totally different than mine.) For me, there was healing in his touches. One day in late December, Micah's friend was visiting from out of town. He had already told me that he was going to go visit him. It wasn't a big deal. But that day had been busy and we hadn't made time to connect. Everything was fine until Micah casually yelled, "Bye," and went out the door.

Instantly I became irrational. That would have been normal for a normal couple under normal circumstances. But in our delicate state, where I required so much (since I was being so needy—there I said it, okay?), I felt hurt and insecure. He had left without what I had gotten used to, a hug or a kiss or even just a reassuring squeeze on my hand or shoulder.

I knew I was overreacting but I really felt my emotions ready to spiral out of control. I had a fear in that moment of reverting back to our other normal, our first marriage. So I decided rather than to spiral, I would sit down and write Micah a letter explaining how I so loved how sweet he was being to me, and how I guess I was still fearful of losing that. I did not want to return to our first marriage. Now that I had been living in our restored marriage, I did not want to return to the old one, which was with little passion, stale, and where love was mainly out of duty, a working partnership.

I had gotten used to baring my soul at that point. Exposing my vulnerabilities was getting to be less and less of a big deal. In the past I may have chosen to sulk for a bit and just be angry until we worked it out (if we left something unresolved), but now I had no desire to let that sit even for a moment.

We decided over communicating was better than not communicating enough. So I put it all out there in a letter. I wasn't even sure I would give it to him, I was just trying to pinpoint where this crazy was coming from and what it was I truly feared. I wrote, "You have completely changed from my first husband. You are sweeter, more thoughtful, and more affectionate. Don't stop. Don't stop pursuing me. Don't stop dating me. I've gotten a taste of your true affections and I want more. I love having a sacred time/space with you where we talk and share our hearts together. I love it when you share your heart with me. Please don't ever close me out again. I want to feel loved by you and I want to know your heart and soul. I guess what I'm saying is, what I want most in this second marriage, is you."

Just as I was in a honeymoon stage with my husband, I was also still in a honeymoon stage with God. There was a new depth to my relationship with him. I was seeking him with a zeal I had left behind years ago. He was meeting with me in our secret place and that became my favorite time of the day. I was learning dependence on him. The whole process for me was exhilarating. It did feel like falling in love for the first time. I was thinking on him in the mornings. I was finding peace and true contentment in his presence as I grew to know him.

Just as I did not want staleness to creep back into my marriage with my husband, I never ever wanted to cut God out of my heart again. I prayed for him not to leave me, just as David did, "Do not cast me from your presence or take your Holy Spirit from me" (Ps. 51:11). As I prayed this, God took me back to the letter I had written Micah that evening. God asked me to reread it, this time reading it as if it had been written by him for me:

*You have completely changed from your old self. You are sweeter, more thoughtful and more affectionate. Don't stop. Don't stop pursuing me. Don't stop dating me. I've gotten a taste of your true affections and I want more. I love having a sacred time/space with you where we talk and share our hearts together. I love it when you share your heart with me. Please don't ever close me out again. I want to feel loved by you and I want to know your heart and soul. I guess what I'm saying is, what I want most in this second marriage, is you.*

I felt fearful in my relationship with my husband that once we were out of the "delicate stage" or "recovery stage" of our relationship, things would go back to the way they had been. Once you reach a certain comfort level, it's human nature to fall back into old habits, to be lax, or not as diligent to keep working on things. I wanted no part of the old ways.

I had already done this once in my relationship with God. It happens when we don't seek him in times of plenty as earnestly as we do in times of want. As he was faithful to me and had given me more than everything I had asked him for, I did not want to enjoy all that he had given me more than I enjoyed simply seeking him.

In that new season, I was seeking God at first only out of desperation to get what I wanted. (That sounds terrible, but it is the truth.) Although he did give me what I was asking him for, in the searching I found true contentment just in his presence alone. He is God. Creator, Void-Filler, Manna-Provider, Healer, Restorer. How could I not fall in love with him as I sought him? How could I not become like an addict wanting more of all of him?

But what was I? How could God ask me to read that letter and tell me it was for me? I knew why I valued my time with him.

It changed me. I needed him. But why would this great God—Creator of everything—value time with *me*? What could I possibly bring to this relationship? Why did he value my affections, my praises? Why did he desire the time I spent in his presence? Why did he want these heart-to-heart times with me?

By looking at my children, I understood how you love beyond reason something you created. My kids formed in my own belly. They are a part of me. An extension of me. I have a stake in them. I have bonded with them. But even understanding the love I have for my own kids still leaves me baffled why this Maker wants intimacy with me. So I gave up on understanding it. Instead I'm learning to accept it. And love it. And crave it. And seek it out.

## • Chapter 27 •

# Lord of the Ring

> *But God demonstrates his own love for us in this:*
> *While we were still sinners, Christ died for us.*
> ROMANS 5:8

I thought Micah was going to give me my ring back when we went to California. That's what I would have done, if I had been in charge of the romance department. We had such a great time that day in San Francisco. There were so many amazing opportunities to re-propose! There was The Palace of Fine Arts, or he could just use the Golden Gate Bridge like he did before. I wasn't picky! We walked along the beach at sunset and it was beautiful. Still the ring was not offered. (And he had it in his backpack the whole time. I checked.) Sure, our marriage wasn't perfect yet, but romance wise, it was as perfect a setting as a Nicholas Sparks novel.

I was sort of devastated when he didn't give me the ring back during that trip. We had oceans in California! *Oceans!* What did we have back home? A paper mill. That's what our city is known for, and the *only* thing it is known for. I was a bit panicked when it was time to go home. I thought if he couldn't decide he wanted to be with me at a place like that, he would never want to be with me. I tried to suppress that dreadful thought, but it entered my mind as we were boarding the plane to return home.

No matter how great our relationship was growing, no ring meant no commitment. I was still waiting. In my mind, it was like we were not even married without it. We finished out our trip, returned back to the airport, and I came home without the ring on my hand.

I did not understand. I was disappointed. But there had been such a change in Micah since this all started that I couldn't deny. I was genuinely feeling love from him. It was enough to make me feel secure even without the ring. It felt ridiculous to worry about a ring when only a few weeks ago, Micah was trying to move out of our house. Now he had had a change of heart, and God was clearly moving and changing him. As thankful as I was to have him returning to me, without my ring being presented back to me, I feared it might all disappear.

I was happy to find that all the progress we made in California did not implode when we returned home. The kids did not go on our trip with us, so naturally it was chaos when we got back. The kids had to get back into their routine. I had to adjust from vacation and having endless "me" time to lack of sleep and messy hair and sticky handprints all over my clothes. It's hard to always feel attractive and pretty when you are wearing peanut butter and applesauce from the waist down, and you have little people shouting out demands like they own you.

I was having a frazzled mommy moment, trying to make sure that homework got done and dinner was on the table, when Micah came into the kitchen with my ring. I had built up this moment in my head so much that when I saw he had the ring in his hand, my first reaction was to refuse it. *No! Not like this! I want the romance and the fairy tale! I want to feel pretty when I get my ring back!* I wanted to have a good story and a Cinderella *before midnight* moment. Her moment happened when she was still gorgeous and having the night of her life, not wearing rags and surrounded by mice!

I don't remember what my exact reaction was, but it was enough to cause Micah to playfully say, "Oh, you don't want it? I thought you did, my mistake. Okay then. . . ." He shrugged his shoulders and started to put it back in his pocket. I had to tackle him to get it back. I was happy. I was aggravated, but happy. Of all the romantic opportunities he'd had! He could've made this really special! He should've outdone himself!

Suddenly he interrupted my thoughts. "I wanted to give it back to you in our daily routine. This is what I am saying yes to. I am saying yes to this, to you, to the kids, to all of it. Yes to our messy lives. It's so easy to make promises on vacation when everything is perfect, without distractions or problems, but that's not real life. This is what I want."

I wish I could say I acted like an adult and appreciated what he was saying right away. But I was stuck on the fact that I was a frazzled mess when he gave me my ring back. I had wanted to take the time to feel pretty, to create this perfect image of a memory we would have forever. The location should have been perfect. I should have looked perfect, with carefully applied makeup, and the perfect clothes, and it should have been in a perfect setting! Maybe I could've snapped a picture of that perfect moment because *it should have been perfect,* darn it!

But evenings in our home with three kids are not perfect. I don't walk around looking amazing and picture-ready! Sometimes it's chaos. It's messy. It's loud. There are distractions everywhere and there is so much that demands my attention. It was actually months later that God showed me the significance in what had happened that evening.

Because Micah "proposed" to me that night, *in the mess,* I can feel confident that at my worst, he's not going to turn around and run, because he made a commitment to me fully seeing it all. It wasn't when I felt perfect. It was when I felt the most imperfect. I felt insecure because of my messy hair and I was frazzled by the kids and my makeup had not been touched up all day!

Ugh! I was a mess!

I bet you already know what God says about that. *How many people* have passed up a "proposal" from God because they felt like they were a mess? We want to wait for the moment when we will feel good and worthy and ready. *If I accept God now, it won't be right, I can't come to him this way, I am a wreck!* I've had friends say to me, "I can't invite God into my heart right now, in the state I am in. I need to get my life together first." I think this is a common notion. We want to "apply our makeup," cover up some stains, at least feel like we look presentable.

I've done that. There have been many a church service where I didn't raise up my hands and worship God like I should and like I genuinely wanted to because I had a bad week and I didn't feel worthy.

Even though I didn't appreciate Micah's tactic at the time he gave me my ring back, it did something to my confidence in our relationship that evening. I don't feel like I have to be perfect in front of him all the time to be loved by him. It was not conditional. He was not asking me to be perfect. He wanted not just the sides of me when I felt my best. He told me he wanted all of it, even our chaos.

Imagine that the same offer is extended to us from God. But this offer is greater because it is not given to us from a man. For as we know people can be temperamental, change their minds, and fail. Jesus died for us while we were still sinners (Romans 5:8), and he draws us in and pursues us when we are "unattractive." Because of who he is, we know we can be confident in his love for us. He wants us. All of us. All the time.

Tackle him, if you must. But take him up on the offer.

# Chapter 28

# Emotions

*My soul is weary with sorrow;*
*strengthen me according to your word.*
PSALM 119:28

January 14 arrived, three months from the day Micah sat me down and told me of his decision to end our marriage. For some reason the three-month anniversary was a very sobering milestone for me. So I intentionally set time aside that day to give thanks to God for all that he had done.

However, for several days beforehand, I had been dealing with overwhelming feelings of sadness. I had been waking up to a somberness, a nagging feeling I couldn't seem to shake. Once again I found myself swatting at "gnats" of sadness and fear, and I constantly had to lock up my thoughts. It was a bit exhausting. As soon as one would be smacked down, I'd be up against another. Before falling asleep at night, I prayed, "God, what is *wrong* with me?"

By now, so many beautiful things had happened. Micah had repented and wanted our marriage to work. We had already taken our emergency anniversary trip to California where God truly began healing our marriage and Micah's heart. He was already treating me with more love and sincerity than I ever recall existing in our "first marriage." So why now—having tasted victory—did I feel sad?

Of course the sadness was related to the affair. Yes, it was past, but the pain of it had resurfaced in my memory. I was sad my husband had been with someone else—just sad that it had happened at all. Sad for all the things that Micah had said and done in those terrible weeks, and all I had endured.

I knew I couldn't walk around in sadness forever. I knew I was being called to let go of it, just as I had been called to put off anything that would hinder me from being obedient to Christ and finishing the race he had set before me. But how was I to do that?

During those few days I wrestled with sadness, I found a folded-up piece of paper in between the seats of my car. They were notes from a Bible study, put there by my friend Rebecca. Rebecca had been in a foreign exchange student program when we were in high school. She lived with me and my family my senior year of high school. We were roommates. We have so many great memories, even going on senior trip together and sharing a beach house for a week. Although from different sides of the world, we became like sisters. She was even there for the prom Micah and I attended that turned out to be our first date!

Having no idea our marriage had just imploded, she planned a trip to come visit us that December. She stayed with us for three weeks. Although we had kept in touch, this visit was the first time I had gotten to see her in ten years. Though I was concerned about the timing of her visit, it ended up being so good for my soul to have her there.

I had just driven her back to the airport earlier in the week, and I was dealing with being sad that she was gone, on top of my feelings of sadness about the affair. I started to feel sorry for myself again. Having her around for nearly a month was so refreshing, even instrumental, but now I felt like I had lost my best friend again.

When I found the crumpled up notes in my car that day I thought she left them there by accident, but later I found out she purposely put them there for me to find! Within the folded-up pages, I found a study on emotions. I found it very fitting since I knew indulging in mine now was out of line. Sadness now was unmerited. I understood that dwelling on the past is just what the enemy would love for me to do. As I had already learned, to wallow in these feelings would not only bring about my own destruction but would also be sin for me.

The study was put together by Rebecca's pastor from Germany, based on a book he was reading by Timothy Jorgensen called *Spirit Life Training*. In it, he claimed that our emotions are the most vocal part of our soul. It explained:

Ungodly emotions will control us. They will put us on a roller coaster of instability in life. They will try to force us to live by their dictates, possess our mouths and wills. Once ungodly emotions rise up to speak through our mouths, that's it. We are finished. We could end up spending years trying to repair the damage that our ungodly emotions just did in only a few moments through our mouths.

Our part is to express and release emotions in a way that is in alignment with God's thoughts and feelings. We are to use our emotions as fuel for good works to the glory of God. When we do that, our emotions can be incredibly effective.[1]

It goes on to suggest that we should train our emotions. We should be able to fire them in the right direction. Our emotions still connect with the spiritual realm. If we simply stop and analyze the source of these feelings, we can become very sharp in the Spirit.

When an emotion comes upon you suddenly, ask God, "Why is this happening? Is it from the Spirit of God, or is it from the devil? Or is it from the spiritual atmosphere of where I am?"

This caught my attention since I had already identified my "sadness" as being the remnants of the enemy's attack. Included in the lesson were practical training tips that I value so much I believe they are worth sharing. There are three keys when dealing with your emotions.

**Doubt them!** Don't let them trick you into a false sense of reality. What we "feel" may not be real. For example, people feel rejection from God when God has not rejected them. God's Word is reality. Emotions, without the Word of God to give them substance, become horrible decision makers.

**Control them!** When we change our focus, we change our feelings every time. If you focus on the negative, the more it will begin to warp your mind and emotions. Focus on the positive, and your emotions will automatically begin to switch direction as well. When emotions are rising, it's prime time for training our emotions. You must do this when your emotions are raging in the opposite direction than they should be, and you don't feel like doing it.

**Seek the face of God!** Constantly seek God's emotions. Stop for a moment and check instantly, "What does the Spirit of God feel? How does God view the situation?"[2]

This information found me in such perfect timing. It was worth gold to me in those days as I was struggling to battle my own emotions. It confirmed all God had been teaching me about my feelings, but to have it in writing that week helped me immeasurably. I carried that paper around with me and reread it whenever I needed the reminder. In a society that encourages us to feel victimized by our circumstances and the feelings that follow, it is liberating to know that we can be free. We don't have to be trapped by our negative feelings. We can take control of them. God has given us the power to overcome even those emotions that come upon us involuntarily.

Another thing that cheered my soul was a verse from the same study. "Why are you down in the dumps, dear soul? Why are you crying the blues? Fix my eyes on God—soon I'll be praising again. He puts a smile on my face. He's my God" (Ps. 42:5 MSG).

That is a psalm of David. As I read through that psalm, I was comforted at the thought of David, *my favorite*, the great hero and man after God's own heart, fighting this battle too. He too had struggled with emotions of sadness. Yet he refused to let lingering emotions of sadness control him.

Just as sure as God meets me and transforms my mind and spirit, he has been providing refuge to his people for all of time. He provides a way of escape from the mental chaos. He brings clarity and peace of mind. My spirit was encouraged. If David battled this, and God helped him, I could battle this too. We served the same God, after all. He doesn't change.

• • •

It seems the common theme I'm finding, even as I gather my thoughts and record all that God has done for me, is that no matter what the hardship, it can be fixed by seeking the face of God. No matter how great the myriad of problems seem, how desperate your situation, how deep your pit, *no matter what the problem*, or what the cause, it can be fixed by fixing our eyes on God.

If this book finds you in your own place of chaos, unrest of soul, uncertainty or sadness, stop reading. My words cannot help you without God's presence and his words being spoken into your heart. Seriously. Stop reading. Go into a quiet place. Shut the door. Shut out the world. Whisper to him. Worship him. Ask the life-giving Creator for help. You are not seeking a mystical power, or a magical or temporary fix. We seek a God who *is*. He is all things and is every answer. And he loves you. So go to him.

# • Chapter 29 •

# *Good Common Sense*

*Dear friend, guard Clear Thinking and Common*
*Sense with your life;*
*don't for a minute lose sight of them.*
*They'll keep your soul alive and well,*
*they'll keep you fit and attractive.*

PROVERBS 3:21–22 MSG

I have talked a lot about spiritual epiphanies, and during this whole journey, I experienced dreams, visions, and miracles. There is no way I would have been able to go through that season of my life without God's supernatural help. Also important and impactful on my journey, however, was something else I received a lot. I received some very good advice, which was also just good common sense. It was not someone just telling me what I wanted to hear to make me feel better in the moment. It was wisdom. I would be remiss if I failed to end this book without giving credit to those things as well.

For some reason when women (and men) find themselves in situations like I found myself in, the advice we get is not always golden. Almost always, even before people hear all the facts surrounding the whole situation, they want to say things like, "You are too good for them! You don't deserve to be treated like that! Move on and don't look back!"

People mean well. They try to build your confidence and make you feel better. They are trying to help you accomplish a "quick fix." They try to tell you that love should be 50/50 *even steven* on both sides and if you are in a relationship where you have to give more than you receive, you must look out for yourself and look for something better.

But we overlook this concept when it comes to our children. I've seen parents deal with their wayward adult children this way. They hate their actions, but love them unconditionally. One-sided love as a parent is completely acceptable. But the moment it becomes unbalanced and not equally reciprocated by a spouse, we are ready to start shoving around divorce papers.

*What in the world is that?* You have promised to stand by this person. My vow was to love and stand by Micah in sickness and in health, for richer or for poorer, for better or for worse. *Not* for better or for worse until this love requires more on my end than you are equally reciprocating to me. What kind of wife would I be to desert Micah in his darkest hour? Even though he had hurt me?

**Advice #1** is this: You made a promise. Keep it. Keep it when it is not glamorous. Keep it when it is not convenient. Keep it when it hurts, and when hanging on seems to be unbearable.

Now, I haven't sought out God on your behalf. I know the instructions he gave me were to stay in the marriage with my husband. I know this because I could hear him in the quiet when I sought him. This leads me to advice #2.

**Advice #2** is: Seek him. Seek Jesus. Find or create a quiet space and learn to tune the well-meaning world out and ask Jesus. He sees the big picture and he is for you.

No matter how much I am for marriage, I can't sit here and advise every woman to stay in their relationships all across the board. My intent is not to heap guilt on anyone who is divorced. I know that marriage is important, but God is a lot more concerned with our hearts and the state of our souls than he is with our marriages. I believe God will even sacrifice a marriage to win one's soul for salvation.

Regardless of the outcome of a broken relationship, whether we stay in the marriage or end up in divorce (since even the Bible permits divorce for certain circumstances), we can still keep our promises. We can walk through tough and even heartbreaking situations with dignity and humility of heart before God, allowing him to heal and empower us along the way. We can be rejected by our spouse and still love him or her. We can walk through a divorce with grace. We can still love, forgive, hope, and all the things of 1 Corinthians 13, despite the outcome of the circumstances.

In fact, in my own trenches, one day it seemed so unhopeful I actually wrote Micah a letter. He seemed determined to divorce me no matter if I agreed or not, so I wrote him a letter telling him that I would be the best ex-wife he could ask for. I told him that I would love him still, even if that love looked differently. I told him I would not fight with him, or say bad things about him to anyone, and that I would forgive him as long as God would continue to give me grace. No matter what the outcome, I determined to keep my promises.

I watched a friend of mine go through a similar struggle. Her husband had been unfaithful. I watched her seek God fiercely, just as I had in my storm, and just like me, she changed. She changed from the initial mad, lunatic, rage-filled woman who could not face her husband without accusing and scolding him for all the things he had done. She began to transform into a softer, gentler, forgiving woman, as she sought the presence of God and asked him for healing and guidance. She surrendered her primal instincts of self-focus and chose a path of love.

Do not think for one second that makes you weak. Walking closely to Jesus will always make you attractive, gentle, grateful, confident, and hopeful. My friend's husband did not stop his pattern of destructive behavior in the marriage. There were things going on in their home that caused her to eventually move out. They went to counseling and communicated certain days of the week while their marriage remained uncertain.

Finally, after months apart, they mutually agreed to divorce. He did not stop the infidelity in the marriage, though he insisted his intentions were to be faithful to his wife. He continued in a pattern of destructive behavior, yet his wife was ultimately able to come to understand that his actions did not define her. She did not need his approval the way she so desperately desired it in the beginning. As God comforted her heart, she began to put the spiritual needs of her husband above her own. She recognized that the void he was seeking to fill could be filled by God alone, and she began praying that God would fill it.

She called me once she made the decision to sign the divorce papers. Although I hate divorce, I am so very proud of my friend. We were two women with very similar situations with two very different outcomes, yet the same outcome that matters. *Jesus.* Seeking him, allowing him to soften our broken hearts and change us into new creations. She achieved the same peace during her divorce that I received in the fulfillment of our marriage being restored.

I could see that God had changed her in her own journey. In the end, she was truly for her husband, even though he had repeatedly hurt her in the course of their marriage. She cried for his salvation and she prayed that he would be able to find strength to overcome the obstacles that kept him from a healthy and happy life, and most of all, that kept him from completely surrendering to God. She was somehow, beyond my understanding, able to be a friend to him when he was in no position to be a husband.

To this day, I am amazed at the work God has done in her life and by her humble obedience. It was a privilege to walk with her through that season, and I know God will not abandon her in the days ahead. *Obedience always puts you in the posture to receive your blessing.*

Who am I to say what path God has for each person? I know that he is God and is not limited to our short list of rules and expectations. My friend was very brave in the face of uncertainty. As she prayed for her marriage, she was like Shadrach, Meshach, and Abednego, who stood tall in the face of King Nebuchadnezzar. When others were bowing they said, "If we are thrown into the blazing furnace, the God we serve is able to deliver us from it, and he will deliver us from Your Majesty's hand. But even if he does not . . . we will not serve your gods or worship the image of gold you have set up" (Dan. 3:17–18).

She was asking God for her marriage, but in the end, even when she didn't get her way as she envisioned it, she remained loyal, faithful, and strong to God. She didn't crumble because she didn't get *her way*. She allowed God to soften her heart, in spite of everything, rather than allowing it to harden like so many do. She even allowed a healthy burden for this man that she had married to form in her heart to intercede for him as she worried that no one else would. She was still fighting for him even after she had given up the dream of having that romantic relationship back. She was fighting very selflessly at that point because she had already lost the marriage.

This, my friends, is a divine work of the heart only God can accomplish. This is love *beyond understanding.*

I am truly thankful for this second chance at life that I now share with my husband. We have now a "second marriage," a fresh start. Still, I know this love story is not only about us. That is secondary, by far. The greatest love story of all is at work here, and is much more glorious and binding, adventurous and exhilarating, than any earthly marriage. Its purpose goes far beyond loving other humans, which is also of great value.

Someone else that I am close to went through an awful divorce a few years back. After about five years of marriage, her husband had started going out more and more often. Sometimes with his wife, sometimes not. He lost interest in the marriage. He began coming home drunk, and his wife could see from their mutual credit cards that he was out at bars and strip clubs into the wee hours of the morning. Finally, he asked for a divorce.

My friend was heartbroken and very determined to make this marriage work. She tried to forgive him for his antics and she was even tolerant of his behavior as she hung on like a mad woman to the marriage. He became cold and hateful to his wife, shutting down any attempts she made at trying to restore the marriage.

She was living out of state and away from all of her family at this time. As a friend, I watched from a distance, horrified as he got a stripper pregnant and moved her into the home he shared with my friend *while my friend still lived there!* I was disgusted by how he could be so insensitive and cruel. My friend had to box up her belongings into the now empty moving boxes of the pregnant stripper who had moved into their bedroom. I cannot make that up. That was her story.

Needless to say, I breathed a sigh of relief when she left the marriage and came home. I share these stories to say that I understand how delicate these situations can be. When I give advice such as, *You made a promise: Keep it,* I also do not mean that all women should stay married regardless of infidelity and abuse. I'm not saying that. I am *not* saying that God will not bless you if you go through a divorce. I've seen, indeed he does.

There are times, like my friends' situations, where I believe God not only *allows* a marriage to come to an end, but *guides* a way out. I understand there are times divorce leads to hope and a new life. Some of the most influential people in my life are products of divorce. God has created beauty out of ruins and blessed second, even third marriages.

So the main point I want to drive home is not whether you should divorce or not. What I am saying is that *we have an obligation to sit before God and listen to what he says about our story.* He is the author of our story, not us. If he says to stay in your marriage (or you can replace the word *marriage* with whatever battle you are trusting God to get you through), you'd better hang on tight. *Don't let go.* Do not use other people's failures to serve as a scapegoat for doing what God has charged you with doing.

I think many a marriage has failed not because it was unfixable, but because we did not put our trust in God that he could reach into our hearts and heal the brokenness. God is the fixer of broken things. Please hear that! Please let that sink in. I wish I could hold your face in my hands and look into your eyes to make you believe this in your heart. *He is the changer of hearts.* We give up on people. God. Does. Not. God heals. He restores. He mends. And please don't ever forget, the bigger our mess, the bigger the stage we have set for him to show off!

**Advice #3.** Your happiness is not the objective. Sometimes we walk through things that do not make us feel good. A lot of people don't like to tell you that, so I will. *That's okay!* We don't need to feel good all the time! We need to place our confidence and worth in a place higher than a man, a woman, or our feelings. I am writing this chapter for those who are going through a tough situation, and no one has told you that it is not about you. I will tell you. It is not all about you.

Just a few days ago someone told me, "I just want you to be happy." This person loves me very much and I appreciate her heart, but as I thought about what she said, I realized that's not the objective. I was not put on this earth to be happy. I believe God does care about my happiness, yes. But there are far more important things I have to do on this earth than be happy. Sometimes God tasks us to do things. He calls us places. He gives us jobs to do that will further his kingdom *at any cost.* He burdens our hearts. *He isn't afraid to let us suffer!* He sees a larger picture and he knows the place we will ultimately reign forever will be *full of happy.* But on this earth, we have a job to do. Happiness is not the number one priority.

When I was interceding for my husband, at the very beginning of all of this when Micah first told me that he was leaving our family, my world stopped. I stepped down from my position in the church. I cancelled my clients. I took the kids out of the activities that had us running all over the place several times a week. I retreated into a place of prayer that secluded me a bit even from my closest friends. That seclusion even has cost me some friends.

I had this picture in my head, you see, that I could not shake. I pictured myself when this life is all over, standing before God on the day of judgment. I envisioned I would extend my arm out to one side as if to display to God all of my accomplishments.

"Here, God," I would say. "Let me draw your attention to all my good deeds." I would proudly show him all of the things I did in my life if I had just kept on going without Micah. Certainly, I had done enough to keep me busy. "Look at all the kids I taught in Sunday school, all the friends I encouraged, how I sacrificed so my kids could be involved in so many sports and activities. All the good things!" *Kingdom* things.

Then I pictured God asking me a question. "Where is your husband? The man I gave to you?"

I would have to respond, "Well, you see, God, I lost him along the way. But look at everything else I've done. Look at all my good things!"

Then God would say, "I gave you *one* person!"

All I could think about was the vow I made when I took Micah as my husband. Mark 10:8 says, "'and the two will become one flesh.' So they are no longer two but one flesh."

The two become one. He is not just any person. He is my person. He is half of *myself*. How could I leave half of myself? Ecclesiastes 4:9–10 NASB says, "Two are better than one. . . . For if either of them falls, the one will lift up his companion. But woe to the one who falls when there is not another to lift him up." If I don't lift him up, who will? *I am the companion!* So I felt if I arrived at judgment without him, I had arrived at best, only fifty percent. I had this feeling that if I gained the whole world, but left him, my priorities would have been off.

At the same conference where this whole story started, there was a session where a Holocaust survivor shared his story. He had known Oscar Schindler personally. He worked in one of Schindler's factories along with his family. He spoke with deepest gratitude and fondness for the man who saved his life.

Schindler, of course, is the real-life hero featured in the movie *Schindler's List*, the German industrialist who took Jewish workers into his factory to keep them out of concentration camps and to save their lives. He started out a powerful and prominent business man, influential and wealthy. Toward the end of his life, he relied on donations of Jewish supporters just to get by, and he died completely broke. By the end of the war, he had literally given everything he had, even offering his possessions as bribes to keep one more Jewish worker out of the death camps.

At the end of the conference session, they handed out buttons for us to take home. On the button was the number one and a quote from Oscar Schindler. It said, "Whoever saves one life, saves the world entire."

I kept this in the forefront of my mind during the fight for my husband in the months ahead.

While I was writing this book, a woman approached me and began to explain to me that God had a big calling on her life and she couldn't just stop everything she was doing for the kingdom (the work she was doing in ministry through her church) just because her husband was struggling with his life and their marriage was on the rocks. I felt that she somehow was seeking my approval to leave her husband so she could be free to go on and do "all the big things" for God. But I couldn't do that. In my own situation, I felt obligated to do quite the opposite. My mind was still ringing with, *Whoever saves one life, saves the world entire.*

How could I tend to anyone else if I was not first looking out for my own? How could I walk into the kingdom of heaven without having done absolutely everything in my power to save the one with whom I had joined my own flesh?

I didn't feel bad about shutting out the rest of the world for a bit to focus my time and energies into interceding for my husband. His salvation and saving my family was my ultimate priority, my highest calling, my greatest role. God prizes their souls as much as any other person, but these folks are mine. *They* are my sphere of influence. I have a spiritual responsibility to care for them.

I kept thinking, *If I don't fight for my husband, for my kids, who will?* I knew that God values the life of *one*, of the four people in my immediate circle, as much as he does thousands of others. They are valuable to God beyond any unit of measurement. He was counting on me to enter into his kingdom one day with *my* people.

**Advice #4.** Remember that you and only you will be the one who has to live for the rest of your life with the choices you make now. Filter the advice you get from those lenses. Try to think about your responses in the moment and how they will affect your life in the long term.

When things fall apart around us, we tend to want to surround ourselves with people and with noise to distract us from being honest with ourselves and dealing with the stuff that hurts.

And let's be honest, the strokes on the back and hearing that it's not our fault, and all of that feels good in the moment. It's a temporary Band-Aid. People tend to tell us what we want to hear in the moment. I am guilty as charged on this one! I've done that in the past.

One of the most helpful things I did was to cut myself out from the world for a bit. I had my Aaron and Hur and a few close friends with whom I only shared things intermittently. Without the clatter of the world trying to sway me in their preferred directions, I was able to seek God in the quiet and hear directly from him. It was also a time of reflection for me, when I could get real with myself.

What did I want? I had to truly ask myself this. No one else, however well-meaning, can answer this question for you. I can see how easy it would be to convince oneself that they want to end a relationship and move on, simply out of pride because they have been rejected. My situation was not only hurtful, but humiliating. I had to swallow my pride if I wanted to be with my husband again.

We also risk being vulnerable to that person and hurting all over again. When dealing with the question of fear and trust, our pastor once said, "Trust is not something you give because it is earned, but rather, look at it as an investment in that person." Investments always involve risk. The fear and hurt was so great in our situation that it would have been easy to convince myself that I just wanted to move on without Micah.

Letting go of him would mean the possibility of falling in love with someone else, someone who had never hurt me. The chance at new love brings an exhilarating, exciting thrill to think about. Maybe the grass would be greener over there. *What possible new romance awaits me?*

Then I had to look at it from the other angle. Micah and I had kids together. He would always be in my life to some measure. He would always be around. People tend to react to things in the moment. *I am hurt now, I must act now, and worry about the future later.* But the future comes all too quickly. I knew that it would find me sooner than I would like, and I would have to live with the way I handled all of this in the moment.

I pictured a few years down the road, divorced and splitting weekends with the kids. I pictured Micah walking up my steps to drop off the kids, and I imagined him giving me a friendly nod and a casual wave good-bye. And then he leaves.

Wait. That's the part I'm not okay with. Every time I see him, what I want, and what I will always want, is to hug him, to kiss his face, to playfully smack him on the backside like I've always done. To embrace him. I can imagine moving on with someone else and knowing he has moved on with someone else, but I would still have the sadness of that loss in the back of my heart, always.

I get the impression the world assumes you are weak when you attempt to fix a broken relationship. As if to "put up with someone" who has clearly wronged you must mean you devalue yourself. But I say, don't be afraid of offering grace. I can tell you that my whole experience has been empowering. Being brave has not made me weak. It has given me a strength I never knew possible. It has given me a faith in God I never knew. I have not been devalued. I've found my value.

I think the world doesn't often encourage us to fight for marriages because they would be asking you to put your heart out there for someone who probably doesn't deserve it. In most love stories portrayed on the big screen, the person who "wins" the love interest at the end was worthy. That's why we root for the happy ending, because they got what they deserved. We carry this over into real life and hope that there is some Mr. Right out there. What we are really saying is, Mr. Perfect, Mr. Worthy, must be out there.

Unfortunately, in real life, none of us are "worthy." We are all flawed. We all make mistakes. Some of us make bigger mistakes than others, but God sees our hearts when they are filthy. He sees into our thoughts the things we pretend aren't there, and still he knows them.

Some unpopular advice that I got early on was from Aunt Jan. She said, "It always takes two people to ruin a marriage. There is never just one person at fault." This sounded offensive at first, especially when Micah's "fault" seemed ginormous and glaring, and at the time I just wanted to point the finger at the obvious problem, infidelity. Still, I took that advice to heart. Without searching my heart and asking God to reveal to me what my part was in all this, I don't think it could be truly mended today.

**Advice #5**. Follow the 1 Corinthians 13 Love Filter. To love with abandon, without concern for yourself, is something that comes from God. God's love has the ability to change you, make you beautiful, attractive, and strong. So be gracious when you judge. Be liberal when you forgive. Filter your love through 1 Corinthians 13, then stand back and watch God do *immeasurably more* than you can ask or imagine.

# • Chapter 30 •

# Immeasurably More

> [He] is able to do immeasurably more than all we ask
> or imagine, according to his power that is at work
> within us.
>
> EPHESIANS 3:20

At some point during the battle for my marriage, my friend Kim and I started sharing our morning devotions with each other. On January 10, she sent me this devotion from *Jesus Calling*:

> Every time you affirm your trust in Me, you put a coin into My treasury. Thus you build up equity in preparation for days of trouble. I keep safely in my heart all trust invested in Me, with interest compounded continuously. The more you trust Me, the more I empower you to do so.
>
> Practice trusting Me during the quiet days, when nothing much seems to be happening. Then when storms come, your trust balance will be sufficient to see you through. Store up for yourself treasure in heaven through placing your trust in Me. This practice will keep you in my peace.[1]

Already that morning I had read Luke 6:38, "Give, and it will be given to you. A good measure, pressed down, shaken together and running over, will be poured into your lap. For with the measure you use, it will be measured to you." I didn't know how to apply that verse to my own life, since we were just about broke financially. But when Kim sent me the devotion about our trust in God being an investment, I went back to my verse of the day and I read it again, this time having in my mind that giving is applicable not only to money, but also to trust.

"Give [trust to God], and it [whatever you are entrusting to him] will be given to you. A good measure, pressed down, shaken together and running over, will be poured into your lap. For with the measure you use, it will be measured to you."

I see a picture of the God of nations, sitting on his eternal throne in heaven, searching the earth, scouring all the tops of human's heads for someone to stand out, to cause him to take notice. I picture him up there watching through the one-way glass of eternity, wondering if anyone will look up from their meaningless routines and think about him.

Then he spots someone approach the glass, examine it curiously, press her nose up against it, and bang on it, trying to see if there's something there. I picture God smacking Simon Peter on the arm and chuckling. "Ha!" he would say. "Did you see that one? She's trying to find me!"

He sees me searching, trying to find something I can't see, so he whispers to me. Just a word or two. But I think I hear something. And I move. I act, just like that. And God gets excited again! "Look at her, Peter!" he says. "She can't even see me, but she is listening!"

So he communicates more. I listen again, and I start running. God jumps up. "Look at her, Peter! She's running ahead full force! She trusts me! She's not stopping."

Then I picture all the chatter in heaven becoming hushed. This eternal God of land and oceans and space and light, gets up off of his throne and stands at the edge of heaven over earth. He starts sprinkling from a gigantic salt shaker. He is shaking something down on me. It's my answer. But it's not *my* answer. Because I couldn't even imagine to ask for this! It's beyond what I even thought to ask for. It's my provision, my life in the reality that is more real than this world. It's my blessing! It's all the good things! And he is sprinkling more than I need. He is sprinkling it until it is "pressed down, shaken together, and running over."

I always felt compelled to believe that God had something up his sleeve for us in that season, beyond just saving our marriage. And indeed, I have already begun to receive my immeasurably more, my good measure, my pressed down, and my shaken together. Because he is able to do *immeasurably more* than all we ask or imagine.

I already shared that Micah was all but spiritually dead at the time of his affair. He was not spending time with God in prayer or reading God's Word. Whatever the things are one must do to remain in relationship with God, he was not doing them. I was sad that he was not acting like the man I had married. But it had been so long since I had seen him filled with a passion and love for God, that I gave up.

One of the things that initially drew me to Micah was his personality. He was fun, easygoing, and patient. He didn't have a bad word to say about anybody. As the years passed, I began noticing subtle changes. Not that he had totally lost those things, but he seemed tightly wound a lot of the time.

Instead of him being playful and fun-loving with the kids, like the kind of dad I had pictured him to be, he became short-tempered and easily aggravated. Being a husband and a dad had become a chore for him rather than a delight. I began overcompensating for his harshness and making up to the kids what I felt they weren't getting from their dad. And I began to correct Micah in front of the kids, undermining him because I didn't have enough patience to talk it over with him in private. That friction greatly contributed to our marital problems.

In this whole mess, I believe Satan planned our destruction, but God allowed the disaster to happen to bring about change. It was as if God was saying to me, "You may think this is acceptable for you, but I am not okay with this life for you. This is not how I created your family to be. If you will just hold my hand through this, I promise I will get you through it. And if you trust me, I promise I will do immeasurably more than you can ask or even imagine."

When I first began to pray for Micah, all I wanted was my husband back. I didn't even think to ask for a better husband! But as Shannon told me, when God restores something, he doesn't return it to how it was; he restores it to its original intent, *how he dreamed it up.* I was too scared to ask for anything more because I had already settled. I was determined to just make the best of it. God said, "No. You don't have to do that. I am *God* after all, the changer of hearts."

My husband who had been disconnected from me, insensitive, impatient with me and the kids, and had buried any dreams he ever had, is a changed man today. I can tell you without any extra fluff, he has restolen my heart. He is tender to me and thoughtful, sweet, and kind. His actions come from a changed heart, from being near to the presence of the living God.

I watch the way he is with the kids now and I am in awe because I have received my heart's desire. It is exactly what I would have asked for had I not been too afraid to ask for it. My faith at the beginning of my mess was pretty low. But after each small victory, my faith increased, and I was able to offer God more trust. And I think trust moves God.

This man who did not even want to come to church with me before, now has his head in God's Word. He is praising God. The person who would just yell at the kids to go to bed, now sits and reads them stories every night and lays hands on them and prays over them. He blesses them and has truly become the leader of our household not out of duty, but out of love. He gets so much joy out of being their dad. This man who once found his identity in his job, now has found his identity in God. He knows that his life serves a greater purpose: to further the kingdom of God.

*What is this? This must have been God's intent for us all along.*

We were sitting on the couch the other night after putting the kids to bed for at least the gazillionth time that night. We could hear them getting back out of bed, thumping around, giggling and talking and things being shuffled around. My blood started to boil. I started to get up and mumbled something about them awakening my wrath, but Micah put his arm on my shoulders and stopped me. He smiled. "No wait. Just listen. We will miss this someday."

Seeing Micah's patience and watching him find enjoyment and pleasure in being a dad is evidence of God working, healing, and restoring. I don't want anyone to read this and think these are small things. They're not. I'm writing this book and I'm oversharing because I don't want anyone to say, "He cheated on his wife and they worked it out. Good job. What's the big deal?"

*No. Listen to me.* It was *so much more* than that. For me, my mountain has been moved. God did not just give me *a man* back. He gave me everything. He first and foremost gave me himself. He could've stopped there. But he did immeasurably more. He went on to restore my husband, his faith, and his heart for me and the boys. He restored our family. He gave me hope, helped me endure, and rescued my soul from the pit.

Realizing who I am in Christ and who Christ is, has been worth this crazy ride. I wouldn't trade it for anything. I want to share it with everyone. Knowing and seeking Jesus is an invitation extended to everyone. An invitation to love. To be loved. To chase after the heart of the only One who can truly fulfill your heart. A beckoning toward adventure. An invitation to obedience.

The human soul works and labors and strives to find happiness.

I am convinced you could have the best job, the most beautiful family, and a six-figure salary, fame, and success, but without the Creator inhabiting the heart of the created, something is going to be lacking. But with God, fulfillment comes.

Today I am living in an aligned reality, the one God dreamed up. His original intent. A good measure, pressed down, shaken together, and running over.

# Notes

## Chapter 9: Breadcrumbs

1. Russell, A. J. *God Calling* (Uhrichsville, OH: Barbour, 1989), October 30. God Calling Devotional app.

## Chapter 11: Exodus

1. Moore, Beth. *Believing God* (Nashville: LifeWay Christian Resources, 2003), DVD.
2. Feinberg, Margaret. *Wonderstruck* (Brentwood, Tennessee: Worthy, 2012), 5.
3. Ibid.

## Chapter 14: New Mercies

1. http://www.dictionary.com/browse/garrison?s=t
2. http://www.dictionary.com/browse/guard?s=t

## Chapter 16: This Is War

1. Young, Sarah. *Jesus Calling* (Nashville: Thomas Nelson, Inc., 2004) January 16. Jesus Calling Devotional app.

## Chapter 17: Up and Running

1. Lewis, C. S. *God in the Dock: Essays on Theology and Ethics* (Grand Rapids, MI: William B. Eerdmans, 2014), 48.

## Chapter 18: Basking

1. http://www.dictionary.com/browse/bask?s=t

2. http://www.dictionary.com/browse/flourish?s=t

3. http://www.dictionary.com/browse/luxuriant?s=t

4. Allen, Jennie. *Chase: A DVD-Based Study* (Nashville: Thomas Nelson, Inc., 2012). DVD.

## Chapter 20: Bluffer

1. Mark Pfeifer, from the sermon titled, "Power in Weakness." Used by permission.

2. http://www.dictionary.com/browse/bluff?s=t

## Chapter 24: Spiritual Warfare

1. http://www.dictionary.com/browse/devour?s=t

## Chapter 28: Emotions

1. Jorgensen, Timothy. *Spirit Life Training* (Shippensburg, PA: Destiny Image, 2011), 59.

2. Concepts taken from Jorgensen, Timothy. *Spirit Life Training* (Shippensburg, PA: Destiny Image, 2011).

## Chapter 30: Immeasurably More

1. Young, Sarah. *Jesus Calling* (Nashville: Nelson, 2004) January 10. Jesus Calling Devotional app.